ULTIMATE SURVIVAL HANDBOOK

Published in 2023 by Welbeck Children's
An Imprint of Welbeck Children's Limited,
part of the Welbeck Publishing Group
Offices in: London - 20 Mortimer Street, London W1T 3JW &
Sydney - 205 Commonwealth Street, Surry Hills 2010
www.welbeckpublishing.com

ISBN: 978 1 83935 224 9

Printed in Heshan, China
1 3 5 7 9 10 8 6 4 2

Author: Andy McNab
Design: Tall Tree Ltd.
Design Manager: Matt Drew
Editorial Manager: Joff Brown
Production: Melanie Robertson

FSC
www.fsc.org
MIX
Paper | Supporting
responsible forestry
FSC® C020056

ULTIMATE SURVIVAL HANDBOOK

SURVIVE IN THE **WILD**, IN THE **CITY** AND **ONLINE!**

ANDY McNAB

WELBECK

CONTENTS

SURVIVING IN THE WILD

SURVIVING IN THE CITY

SURVIVING ONLINE

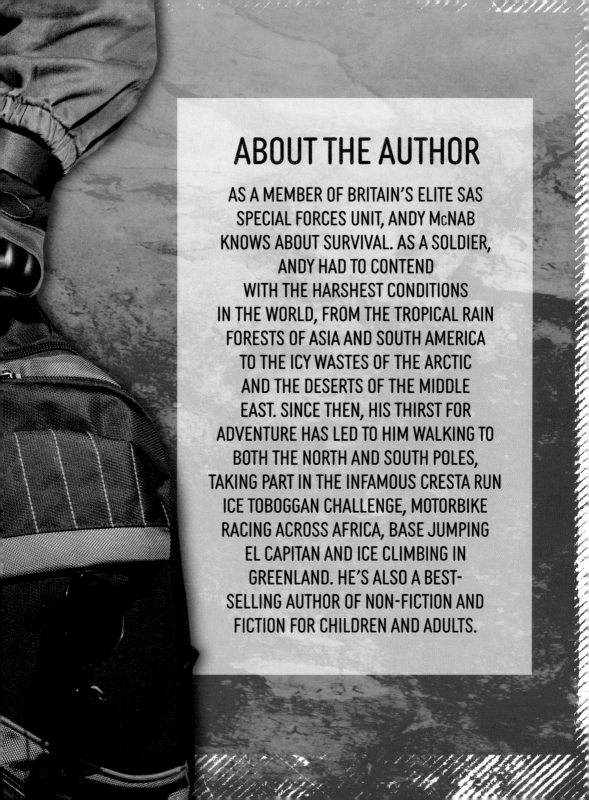

ABOUT THE AUTHOR

AS A MEMBER OF BRITAIN'S ELITE SAS SPECIAL FORCES UNIT, ANDY McNAB KNOWS ABOUT SURVIVAL. AS A SOLDIER, ANDY HAD TO CONTEND WITH THE HARSHEST CONDITIONS IN THE WORLD, FROM THE TROPICAL RAIN FORESTS OF ASIA AND SOUTH AMERICA TO THE ICY WASTES OF THE ARCTIC AND THE DESERTS OF THE MIDDLE EAST. SINCE THEN, HIS THIRST FOR ADVENTURE HAS LED TO HIM WALKING TO BOTH THE NORTH AND SOUTH POLES, TAKING PART IN THE INFAMOUS CRESTA RUN ICE TOBOGGAN CHALLENGE, MOTORBIKE RACING ACROSS AFRICA, BASE JUMPING EL CAPITAN AND ICE CLIMBING IN GREENLAND. HE'S ALSO A BEST-SELLING AUTHOR OF NON-FICTION AND FICTION FOR CHILDREN AND ADULTS.

STAY SAFE, STAY READY!

THIS BOOK CONTAINS INFORMATION that can be invaluable in dealing with a sudden emergency, in the wilderness or elsewhere. As well important knowledge about fundamental survival rules and techniques, you'll also find true-life stories of survival inside.

REMEMBER, IT'S JUST AS IMPORTANT to stay safe in an urban environment as it is in the great outdoors. And even when you're online, you need to make sure that your information and privacy are protected. This book contains everything you need to know to make yourself street-smart and safe in every environment.

WHEN YOU UNDERSTAND THESE RULES AND TIPS, you'll be safe and ready—whether it's in the wild, in the city, or online!

SURVIVING IN THE WILD

PREPARATION

ACCIDENTS CAN HAPPEN ANY TIME, ANY PLACE, TO ANYONE.
FAIL TO PLAN AND YOU PLAN TO FAIL!

THE 3 Ps

THE THREE MOST IMPORTANT SURVIVAL WORDS
• PLANNING • PREPARATION • PACKING

PLAN your activity carefully. Ask yourself lots of "what ifs." What if you get lost? What if it gets too dark to continue? What if you or one of your friends twists an ankle? If you've started your trip and things aren't going the way you planned, you should always stop, think, and weigh things up—and never be afraid to turn back.

PREPARE for the worst and hope for the best! One of the most crucial things to do before you set off is to let people know where you're going, and just as important, when you'll be back. Leave a plan of your trip with family or a trusted adult. If you're hiking with friends or family for several days in the wilderness, tell local services, such as a park ranger.

FIRST-LINE EMERGENCY KIT

Your first-line emergency kit when you go into the wilderness should be:

- a map (preferably in a waterproof case)
- a whistle
- a compass
- a headlamp (tape a spare set of batteries to the headband)

- a lighter, if you're allowed one; if not, a fire-steel

. . . all of which you can wear around your neck on a lanyard (paracord is good for this, as it has so many other uses).

You should also have:

- space blanket or emergency bivvi bag

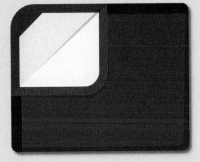

Buy the best equipment you can afford. It will work better and last longer.

- mobile phone
- water bottle
- survival kit—you can buy ready-made survival kits, or you can make up your own.

PACK wisely. If you're off on an outdoor adventure you should carry as little weight as you possibly can. That means that if you're already carrying a tent and sleeping bag, and maybe a camping stove and cooking gear, you should add just the bare essentials to keep you warm, dry and comfortable—and, if there's an emergency, safe.

WHAT TO TAKE

FIRST AID KIT: You can buy a good first aid kit at any pharmacy or camping store, but if you make up your own make sure it contains at least these items:

- ROLLED BANDAGE
- TRIANGULAR BANDAGE
- SCISSORS
- TWEEZERS
- SAFETY PINS
- ANTIBIOTIC EYE OINTMENT
- BLISTER PADS AND WATERPROOF ADHESIVE BANDAGES
- SMALL ROLL OF ZINC OXIDE TAPE
- PLAIN GAUZE PAD, 150 MM x 900 MM (6 IN x 35 IN)
- A CAN OF SPRAY BANDAGE TO SEAL SMALL CUTS AND GRAZES

CELL PHONE: Protect your cell phone with a waterproof case and pack a back-up power pack or a solar-powered charger.

CLOTHING: Several light layers are better than one heavy layer. You can take them off or put them on to regulate your temperature. One essential piece of gear is a warm, waterproof, lightweight jacket.

SOCKS: Good socks prevent blisters. They also keep your feet warm and dry.

SLEEPING BAG: Your sleeping bag should have enough padding to keep you warm at night even without a tent. It should never be allowed to get wet, so always pack it inside a waterproof cover—preferably two.

TENT: Some kind of shelter from the elements is essential for long-term survival. Which tent you choose will depend on the weather conditions you predict and how much you can afford to spend.

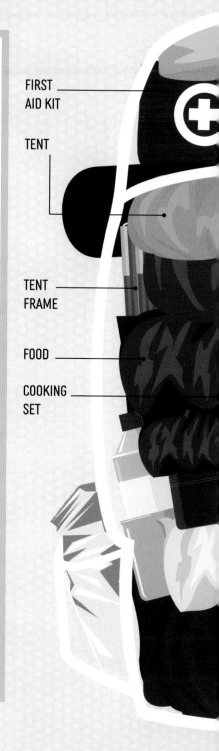

FIRST AID KIT

TENT

TENT FRAME

FOOD

COOKING SET

JACKET

HEADLAMP

MATTRESS PAD

WATER

SLEEPING BAG

PACKING A BACKPACK

Carry only what you need! If you're in a group, you can share many communal items.

BOTTOM

Pack the items you'll use least, which might include your sleeping bag, pillow, a towel and emergency rations.

MIDDLE

Add your heaviest items to the center. These will include water, food, cooking equipment and maybe a tent. Packing them close to your back in the center of the bag gives you good balance. Finish the center section by adding your lightest items farthest from your back.

TOP

Finish by adding all the essential items you use most often. These will include a flashlight, first-aid kit, map and snacks, and also your box or bag of second-line emergency gear. Be careful as too much weight at the top will throw you off balance.

EXTERIOR

Don't overdo it with items hanging from the pack's exterior. These can snag on branches or throw you off balance.

"

ANDY SAYS

Use the buddy-buddy system.
To prevent any strains or injuries, your buddy lifts your backpack onto your back, and you lift their backpack onto theirs.

"

FINDING YOUR BEARINGS

IF YOU GET LOST, YOU NEED TO TAKE STOCK AND WORK OUT WHERE YOU ARE.

STOP!

As soon as you realize you're lost, the important thing is to STOP. STOP stands for Stop, Think, Observe, Plan.

STOP: Don't panic. Panic will make you push on deeper and deeper into the forest or jungle and get more and more lost.

THINK: Find somewhere nice to sit down, take a couple of deep breaths, and try to figure out where you went wrong, and whether it's best to retrace your steps. Contact people by phone if you have one and there is signal.

OBSERVE: Do you have a map? Look around for landmarks. Can you dig a snow shelter? Can you hear a river, which you could follow downstream until you find people? Is there a big open space where you can build a signal fire or mark out an SOS?

PLAN: If night is falling, sleep on it. What do you need to do first? In the morning, if you do decide to leave, mark your trail somehow, so if your plan doesn't work out, at least you can retrace your steps.

TIP — If you're lost in woods and you find a track that then forks (with you at the stem of the "Y"), you're probably going deeper into the forest. Retrace your steps.

USING YOUR WATCH

If you have a watch with hands, you can determine direction by pointing the hour hand directly towards the sun (or, in cloudy conditions, towards the area of brightest light).

Divide the angle between the hour hand and 12:00 by two, and you have south (or north in the southern hemisphere). Alternatively, draw a conventional watch face on the ground, with the hour hand pointing at the sun, and do as above.

FINDING DIRECTION AT NIGHT

In the Northern Hemisphere, the North Star is the most accurate natural guide available. To find it, first search for the Big Dipper (or Plough). The two stars that form the side of the saucepan farthest from the handle are the pointers: extend the line formed by them for roughly five times its length, and you will see the North Star. That is the direction north.

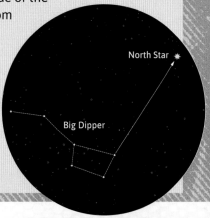

North Star

Big Dipper

HOW TO IMPROVISE A COMPASS

YOU WILL NEED
A CUP OF WATER OR A PUDDLE • A LEAF • A SEWING NEEDLE OR BOBBY PIN

Lay the leaf in the water and gently place the needle on top of the leaf.

▼

It will then start spinning before settling and staying still.

▼

The direction in which the needle is pointing will be along the north–south line.

ANDY SAYS

You can greatly improve the needle's efficiency by stroking it with a magnet. There is a tiny magnet behind the speaker of a mobile phone!

SURVIVING THE COLD

IN THE EXTREME COLD, CONSERVE YOUR BODY HEAT TO AVOID HYPOTHERMIA, A POTENTIALLY DEADLY CONDITION.

SPOTTING HYPOTHERMIA

THE FIRST SIGN of hypothermia is shivering, which is the body trying to warm itself. Shivering might start mild then become more aggressive, then eventually it will stop altogether.

"THE UMBLES": mumbles, stumbles, fumbles, and grumbles. Hypothermia victims may slur their speech, become confused, and lose their coordination. They will eventually become apathetic and irrational. That is a sure danger sign.

TREATING HYPOTHERMIA

Once your body loses its ability to reheat itself, your only hope is to add heat.

Replace the victim's wet base layers with dry clothing. If they are conscious, feed them calorific drinks and food and have them exercise in short bursts. Avoid alcohol and caffeine.

If the victim is unconscious, put them in a sleeping bag if you have one, and insulate them from the cold ground. If possible, wrap them in a survival blanket, tarp, or plastic sheet.

Sharing body heat with skin-to-skin contact can also be a good way to warm up a hypothermic victim.

HOW THE BODY LOSES HEAT

1. EVAPORATION	2. RADIATION	3. CONDUCTION	4. CONVECTION
Moisture and heat leave the body when we sweat and breathe.	When the body is warmer than the outside temperature, heat leaves the body.	Body heat flows into objects in contact with the body (clothing, air, water).	Moving air (the wind, for example) transports heat away from the body.

PREVENTING HYPOTHERMIA

To prevent hypothermia, you need to minimize heat loss.

DO: Get out of the wind and stay dry.

DO: Put on extra clothing (if you have any) before you start to shiver.

DO: Light a fire at the first hint of a chill; if possible, get more than one fire going, so you can heat yourself from more than one side.

DO: Drink as much hot fluid as you can. If you have spare food, use it to refuel by eating little and often.

DO: Add insulation. Use anything at hand, including dry plant material or even the stuffing inside car seats.

DON'T: Sit on or lean against rocks or metal—you will lose heat very rapidly through conduction.

DON'T: Eat snow. It not only takes body heat to melt the stuff, but it cools the body from the inside.

ANDY SAYS

Check, re-check, then check again that you're not losing heat through evaporation, radiation, conduction or convection.

SURVIVING THE HEAT

WATCH OUT FOR HEAT EXHAUSTION, WHICH OCCURS WHEN YOUR BODY IS UNABLE TO COOL ITSELF. IT CAN DEVELOP INTO DEADLY HEATSTROKE.

HEAT EXHAUSTION

The symptoms of heat exhaustion include profuse sweating, pale skin, weakness, nausea, vomiting, headaches, and muscle cramps.

TO TREAT HEAT EXHAUSTION, get the victim to a cool shady location and let them rest. Lay them down and elevate their legs slightly. Give them sips of cool water or an electrolyte solution and help them to cool down with a wet bandana on their forehead.

HEAT CRAMPS

When you sweat, you lose not only water but also essential body salts.

Called electrolytes, these salts aid electrical nerve impulses to your muscles. Even if you're drinking plenty of water, a lack of salt can cause your muscles to cramp. Avoid cramps the same way you would avoid heat exhaustion—by not exerting yourself.

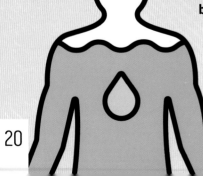

HEATSTROKE

Heat exhaustion can develop into potentially lethal heatstroke. The skin of someone experiencing heatstroke will often be dry and red hot to the touch.

▼

Look out for symptoms including nausea, vomiting, rapid breathing and heartbeat, throbbing headaches, confusion, and unconsciousness.

▼

They need to be cooled immediately. Get them to a shady area, remove any clothing that stops their body from breathing, such as a leather or nylon jacket, and cool their body with cold water and wet clothes. Focus on the head, neck, armpits, and groin.

AVOIDING HEATSTROKE

GET OUT OF THE SUN

Move into the shade of a vehicle, tree, some bushes, a rock—anything around.

LIMIT EXERCISE

Your walking distance limit in the heat of the day is 1,500 feet (500 m). Don't exert yourself physically until nightfall.

DON'T UNDRESS

Do not take all your clothes off as you sweat more without your clothes on. You can't afford to lose any precious water from your body. Only discard clothes that don't allow your body to breathe.

AVOIDING DEHYDRATION

You can become dehydrated in the middle of an Arctic winter just the same as the middle of the day in the Sahara.

Thirst is indicative that you need more water. Other symptoms are a feeling of discomfort, a slow-down in movement, redness in the face, impatience, loss of appetite, and rapid pulse and breathing.

There is little you can do to stop yourself from losing as much as 4 pints (2 liters) of water a day from urination, bowel movements, and breathing. But you can reduce your losses in other areas. Unless you have lots of water available, eat as little as possible and ration your sweat.

21

MAKE A SHELTER

TO AVOID HYPOTHERMIA OR HEAT EXHAUSTION, YOU MUST PROTECT YOURSELF FROM THE ELEMENTS AS QUICKLY AS POSSIBLE. CHOOSE A SHELTER THAT WILL GET YOU OUT OF THE WEATHER MOST QUICKLY.

KEEP IT SIMPLE

THE MOST OBVIOUS READY-MADE shelters in many survival situations are vehicles: cars, boats, and planes. Natural, ready-made shelters include rocky overhangs, trees and caves.

IF YOU HAVE TO BUILD a shelter, choose the smallest, easiest, and most effective one that can be made with the materials available. Above all, conserve your energy when building it: no need for elegant log cabins when a simple lean-to will do.

MAKE A LEAN-TO

A lean-to is a sloping roof that extends to the ground. It needs to be steep enough (60°) to shed rain, high enough to let you sit, and wide enough to let you stretch out.

Position the lean-to so that you are protected from the wind and can light a fire in front of it. Don't make your lean-to more elaborate than you have to. All you need is a pole long enough to stretch between two trees and two other poles with forked ends.

This trick will save you hours of work. Hold the first pole against the trees at the right height, rest one forked pole against one end of it, and the other forked pole at the other. The structure will support itself. You now have the basic framework for your roof.

Thatch the lean-to with branches, foliage, moss, earth, or snow. Best are fir boughs, laid like tiles on a roof, starting with the bottom row and working upward. Lay the boughs upside down, and with the undersides of the leaves or needles uppermost. Insulate the floor with leaves, dead pine needles, and more boughs. Then drive two sticks into the ground, about 3 feet (1 m) from the entrance. Use these as a prop for two or three large logs piled one on top of the other. This is the reflector for your fire.

23

SHELTERING IN THE SNOW

When heavy snow falls in coniferous forests, there is not much drifting and the snow stays light, powdery, and uniformly deep.

Natural shelters are built at the base of thick evergreens with low branches, in the form of a "well" in the deep snow at the base of the tree trunk. If you need a winter shelter fast, this kind is unbeatable.

It is impossible to exaggerate the importance of insulation. You will need bedding that is at least 1 foot (30 cm) thick between you and the ground.

BUILDING A SNOW CAVE

YOU WILL NEED
- A SHOVEL • AN ANORAK • A PLASTIC BAG

Choose a big drift of packed snow. The best location for a snow cave is in a drift with a fairly steep face, greater than 30°. This will ensure that there is sufficient depth of snow.

▼

Mark your cave site to prevent anyone falling on top of you while digging. Probe for trees or other obstacles, then dig.

▼

Although the final entrance should be small, it is best to make this larger to start off with and fill it in later. Dig a deep slot into the drift, high and wide enough to allow you to work upright.

▼

Excavate the snow on either side of the slot to create an open living area. For maximum insulation and structural stability, the walls and ceiling should be at least 2 feet (60 cm) thick.

KEEPING WARM

STRIP OFF

Digging is hard work and the effort will make you work up quite a sweat. Only dry clothing will keep you warm during the night ahead. So strip off while you're digging.

BEDDING

SHAPE A BED PLATFORM ABOUT 20 INCHES (50 CM) HIGH. DON'T BUILD A PALACE. THE SMALLER THE AREA TO BE HEATED THE BETTER. INSULATE YOUR BED WITH BOUGHS OR ANYTHING AT HAND. DON'T JUST INSULATE YOUR SHELTER—INSULATE YOURSELF! STUFF YOUR CLOTHES WITH DRIED GRASS AND LEAVES.

CANDLE HEAT

A single candle will provide ample heat. In fact, it may be too hot, and make the roof drip or sag. You can cut down on dripping by making the roof as dome-shaped as possible and by glazing the inner surfaces with the candle flame. If any drips develop, dab on a handful of snow.

MAKING FIRE

A GOOD FIRE NOT ONLY PROTECTS YOUR BODY FROM THE COLD, IT ALSO PROTECTS YOUR MIND AND DRIVES AWAY LONELINESS AND FEAR.

1 BEFORE YOU START

Build a fire the moment your shelter has a roof. That way, if darkness falls, at least you know you'll have some shelter and a fire, rather than just a well-built shelter but no fire.

Logs

Kindling

Twigs

You build a fire in stages, you don't just light one. You will need tinder (material that is very easy to burn), kindling (such as twigs, small enough to be burned by the tinder), fuel (a range of larger pieces of wood and other materials, up to big log size), and, of course, a lighter.

Gather your kindling and fuel. Lots of it. Work out how many branches and logs you think your fire will burn, then double it. Then add a few more logs for luck. As you gather your kindling, store it carefully in case it starts to rain or snow. Stack all the larger pieces well within arm's reach when you're lying in your shelter.

ANDY SAYS

Fires don't burn solids, they burn gases. To vaporize large logs, you need a lot of heat generated from the kindling and tinder.

Make sure your wood you collect is dry. Wet wood will be harder to burn and create more smoke.

2 PREPARING THE SITE

YOU WILL NEED
2 STAKES • 3 LOGS • HANDFUL OF STONES

Drive two stakes into the ground behind the fire site at an angle away from it. Pile two or three big logs against it as your fire reflector. If your shelter is a lean-to you're lying lengthwise in, try to make your reflector about 6 feet (2 m) long.

▼

Lay two long, thick logs or branches parallel to each other, about 20 inches (50 cm) apart, in front of your shelter. As your fire burns, you can make it spread between the logs until it's heating the whole length of your body.

▼

If there are dry rocks nearby, make a ring of them to contain your fire. If the fire goes out for any reason, you can bring the hot stones into your shelter with you for extra warmth.

This site has a fire reflector (the silver sheet attached to the roof) to reflect the fire's heat.

WHAT TO BURN

NATURAL TINDERS

- Birch bark
- Resin shavings
- Pitch shavings
- Cedar bark
- Dry tree moss
- Dry pine needles
- Dry leaves
- Rotten wood
- The nests of birds
- Termites' nests
- Dead bamboo
- Fine down from the breasts of birds
- Dry grass
- Your own hair (if you're really stuck)

MAN-MADE TINDERS

- Cotton wool balls greased with Vaseline
- Candle stubs, insect repellent
- Doritos, or other corn chips
- Cotton wool
- Scorched cloth

Pine cones   Corn chips

FUEL
DON'T FEEL RESTRICTED TO WOOD AS A FUEL FOR YOUR FIRE. IF DRY ANIMAL DUNG, A SPARE TIRE, MATS OR GASOLINE FROM YOUR CAR ARE ALL YOU HAVE, USE THEM.

TEEPEE

The basic way of starting fires is the "teepee"—although it does have a tendency to collapse. Build a little teepee of thin, delicate twigs around your tinder. When there is sufficient heat, add bigger twigs.

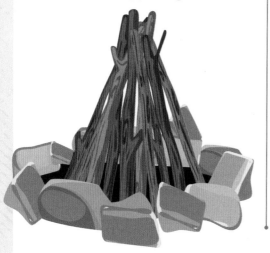

LOG CABIN

The "log cabin" takes a bit longer to build, but is more stable. Make it by laying a log on each side of a tinder and kindling teepee. Put two more logs across the ends of the first two and continue upward. **Slant the "walls" inward slightly.**

✚ START A FIRE WITH ✚ FIRST-AID KIT ITEMS

Alcohol-based hand sanitizers contain a high percentage of ethanol, a highly flammable substance. Squirt some onto wood and ignite it with a match or lighter. Ethanol burns with a blue flame that is not always visible. Hold a couple of sticks above it for a few seconds and before you know it, you will have a fire.

The best source of ignition for lighting your fire is a lighter or matches. However, if you don't have those items and the sun is shining you can use:

A CONVEX LENS will set tinder smoldering if the sun is strong enough. Any single eyeglasses lens can be tried, as can a gun-sight lens, the magnifying glass on a Silva compass, a camera lens, or a binocular lens.

CONCAVE MIRRORS will also work. These can be mirrors from car headlights, plane landing sights, even a shaving mirror—the larger the better. You can improvise a concave mirror by polishing the bottom of a drinks can with sand or soil.

A CLEAR PLASTIC BOTTLE FULL OF WATER can be used as a magnifying glass to focus the sun's rays on your tinder.

If the sun isn't shining, you can use:

A PIECE OF STEEL struck hard against a flint or stone.

A BATTERY. Put both contacts of a 9-volt battery against a pinch of steel wool to create a short circuit and a spark.

Alternatively, use the tinfoil wrapper of a chocolate bar to create the short circuit.

29

FINDING WATER

DRINKING WATER IS ESSENTIAL TO SURVIVAL. YOU CAN LAST AN ABSOLUTE MAXIMUM OF TEN DAYS WITHOUT IT. YOUR NEED FOR WATER TAKES PRECEDENCE OVER YOUR NEED FOR FOOD.

FOLLOW THE ANIMALS

Although some animals are able to obtain moisture just from their food, the majority need water if they are to survive.

IF AN ANIMAL TRAIL shows fresh signs of use, following it might lead you to water.

ALL SEED-EATING BIRDS
need a supply of water. Flocks of finches or other birds seen feeding on grass seeds are a sure indication that water is nearby.

SOME OF THE MORE HIGHLY ORGANIZED INSECT
communities such as bees and ants need water. They may lead you to their supply, however small it is.

SOURCES OF WATER

Many plants with fleshy leaves or stems store drinkable water. Trying them is the way to find out. Tying a plastic bag around a leafy branch can often yield as much as one cup (240 ml) of dew.

CLIMBING VINES in tropical forests yield a large amount of fluid, but make sure it is not milky. Cut lengths of vines and hold them above your mouth.

ALONG THE SEASHORE, water can be found in the dunes above the beach.

RAIN is an obvious source of water. Scrape a depression in the ground as a catchment area, and line it with a waterproof coat, plastic sheet, or leaves.

CAVES, particularly limestone caves, sometimes contain streams or pools.

HARVEST WATER from birch sap, especially in the early spring. Make a knife slash on the bark in the shape of a "V." The sap will trickle out.

IS IT SAFE?

TEST FOR FRESHNESS

The danger signs in water are: lack of insect life; absence of animals or animal tracks; and a white coating on the rocks or ground around the water.

One interesting test for the freshness of water is to wiggle your finger in your ear and pull out a bit of wax. Drop this into the water. If the water is fresh, the wax will settle to the bottom. If the water is iffy, the wax will form an oily sheen on the surface.

IF THE WATER LOOKS BAD…

If the water does look bad, pull a piece of cloth tight over your mouth and put your face down in the water and suck. If you have the materials, filter the water through a sock which has six alternate layers of charcoal and sand, then boil for two minutes.

Under no circumstances must you drink sea water. Its salt concentration is so high that body fluids must be drawn to eliminate it.

IN THE COLD

FORCE YOURSELF TO DRINK WATER UNDER COLD CLIMATIC CONDITIONS, EVEN IF YOU THINK YOU DON'T NEED IT. MELT SNOW OR ICE FIRST.

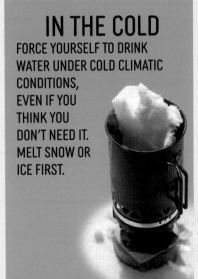

MAKE A SOLAR STILL

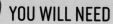

YOU WILL NEED
• A SHOVEL • PLASTIC SHEETING • BUCKET OR CUP

In deserts and very dry areas, water may be present in the ground. If you have a piece of plastic sheeting, you can rig up a very effective still to produce water by condensation.

Dig a hole about 3 feet (1 m) across and 3 feet deep. At the bottom, place a bucket, cup, or improvised container. Place vegetation around it—sliced up, shredded, or broken up.

▼

Pour over the vegetation any polluted fluid you have available. Cover the hole with a large plastic sheet, allowing it to sag down until it is just an inch or two from the container, but not touching the sides of the hole or the vegetation.

▼

Put a small stone wrapped in cloth in the center of the sheet, so that it keeps a taut, inverted-cone shape. If you have a length of rubber tubing, put it into the container and lead it out under one edge of the sheet. Anchor the edges of the sheet with rocks and sand or earth to make it as watertight as possible.

▼

A solar still should produce at least 1 pint (half a liter) of water per day. If you have more plastic, make more stills. Your still may also become a source of food: the water container attracts snakes and small animals, which slide under the plastic then cannot climb out again.

TIP You may have few choices for the site of a solar still. But the best locations for digging the pit are in a riverbed (whether or not there is surface moisture), where there are signs of moisture, or where there is vegetation. Clay soil holds more moisture than sandy soil. Any site you choose must be free of shade: the still only functions when exposed to the sun.

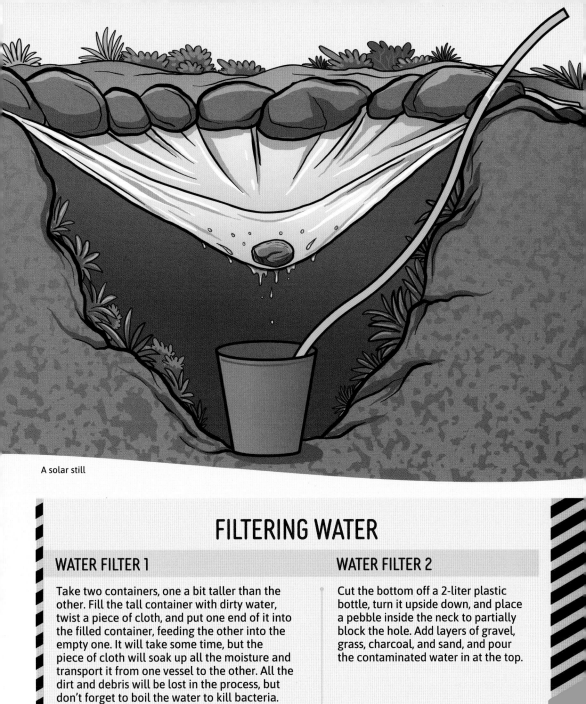

A solar still

FILTERING WATER

WATER FILTER 1

Take two containers, one a bit taller than the other. Fill the tall container with dirty water, twist a piece of cloth, and put one end of it into the filled container, feeding the other into the empty one. It will take some time, but the piece of cloth will soak up all the moisture and transport it from one vessel to the other. All the dirt and debris will be lost in the process, but don't forget to boil the water to kill bacteria.

WATER FILTER 2

Cut the bottom off a 2-liter plastic bottle, turn it upside down, and place a pebble inside the neck to partially block the hole. Add layers of gravel, grass, charcoal, and sand, and pour the contaminated water in at the top.

FINDING FOOD

THERE ARE OFTEN PLENTY OF OPTIONS, BUT
CHOOSE YOUR SOURCES OF FOOD CAREFULLY.

PLANTS

Plants are likely to be your most important food in a survival situation, for the simple reason that they don't run away.

DON'T eat white, yellow, or red berries.

DON'T eat anything that looks like beans or peas. They are often toxic.

DON'T eat bulbs, unless they look, smell, and taste like onions or garlic.

DON'T eat plants that look very brightly colored or simply weird.

DON'T eat any plant that irritates your skin when you touch it.

DON'T eat fungi, unless you're an expert.

DON'T eat any plant with a milky sap, except for dandelions.

DON'T eat any plant with umbrella-shaped blossoms.

DON'T eat anything that resembles a cucumber, melon, dill, parsley, or tomato.

FOOD THAT RUNS AWAY

It's safe to eat the flesh of all mammals when it's fresh and unspoiled. The offal, or innards, of all mammals is edible, too, except the livers of seals or polar bears, which hold a poisonous amount of vitamin A. It's safe to eat the flesh of all birds. Their eggs are also edible. It's safe to eat lizards, snakes, frogs, and salamanders, but skin them first.

INSECTS AND GRUBS

THE BENEFITS OF EATING CRUNCHY CRITTERS
• FOUND EVERYWHERE • TASTY • NUTRITIOUS • A RELIABLE FOOD SOURCE…HOWEVER…

Eat only fresh insects.

▼

Don't eat brightly colored insects—they are probably toxic.

▼

Don't eat pupae found in the soil.

▼

Don't eat eat hairy caterpillars—they sting.

Insects and grubs are an excellent source of protein.

TIP A fire at night will attract various night-flying insects. So will a flashlight or lantern. Look in the branches and hollow trunks of trees. Turn over stones and debris and tear open hollow logs. Many insects, such as grasshoppers, are best collected at night or in the early morning while they are still lethargic.

COOKING YOUR FOOD

Boiling is by far the best way because it preserves natural juices and vitamins. Steaming works well for shellfish.

To roast fish, small mammals, and other food, roll them in mud or clay and cook them in hot coals. When roasting, there is no need to scale fish or to skin animals—when you remove the clay the scales or skin will peel away with it.

FISHING

There are no known poisonous freshwater fish anywhere in the world. Only catch the amount of fish that you need as it goes bad quickly. Remember that you are not fishing for trophies—a small fish is better than nothing.

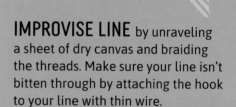

You can sometimes find fish under the banks of a river. If you find one:

TICKLE ITS BELLY and feel for the gills. While tickling, pinch the gills and flip the fish out of the water. The best place to try this is under the branches of overhanging trees.

LIGHT ATTRACTS FISH. Flying fish can be landed on a raft by reflecting flashlight or moonlight on a shirt and catching them as they jump. Or reflect moonlight with a mirror on the riverbed—the fish will lie over it.

EXPERIMENT with different lures—feathers, bits of plastic, buttons, keys, coins, bright cloth, fish entrails, slivers of fish flesh, small shells.

IMPROVISE LINE by unraveling a sheet of dry canvas and braiding the threads. Make sure your line isn't bitten through by attaching the hook to your line with thin wire.

HOOKS can be made from bone and wood, as well as bent pins, ring-pulls, safety pins or small pen-knives with the blade tied at an angle.

TRY A SKEWER HOOK. Tie the line around it halfway along its length, then lay the skewer along the line. Feed bait over skewer and line. When the fish takes the bait, jerk the line. The skewer will open out and jam in its stomach.

MAKE A FISH TRAP

YOU WILL NEED
• 2-LITER PLASTIC BOTTLE • BAIT • FISHING LINE • PENKNIFE

Use the penknife to cut the bottle in two, just below the shoulder, where the top stops curving.

▼

Now put some bait in the bottom section.

▼

Take the top section and insert it into the bottom section so the neck faces the bottom, then tie the two pieces together. If possible, one of the ties should be extended so you can anchor the trap to a branch.

▼

Hold the trap under the water so it fills and sinks. Check it regularly and replace the bait. Anything you catch will be small, but in sufficient numbers they will make a meal. Your catch can also be used as bait.

SAFETY RULES FOR EATING FISH

Don't eat any fish that does not look, feel, or smell right. In the tropics, fish can go off even minutes after death, so make sure you cook it at once.

• If you squeeze a fish and the indentations remain, forget it.
• If the fish's eyes are milky, forget it.
• If the fish doesn't have scales, forget it.
• Don't eat any fish that doesn't look like a fish. This includes fish shaped like a box, fish that inflate themselves after being caught, fish with a snout-like mouth, or fish that look like a rough stone.
• Don't touch any conical or spindle-shaped shellfish.
• Never eat fish offal. Use it as bait instead.

SURVIVING IN THE DESERT

DESERTS ARE HARSH PLACES—BOILING HOT DURING THE DAY, FREEZING COLD AT NIGHT. YOU NEED SHELTER AND WATER, AND TO BE RESCUED.

SANDSTORMS

Sandstorms can last from a few hours to several days. If a huge black cloud blots out the sun and the sky and air become yellow and dusty, find shelter or hunker down, cover your face, and wrap yourself up as best you can. Use your gear as a shield for your head.

Rocks and other dangerous debris can be carried along in a sandstorm.

➕ IMMEDIATE ACTIONS

If you are stuck in the desert, it is vital to get out of the sun. Get into the shade of a tree, some bushes, a rock, a vehicle—anything, as long as it's nearby and you don't have to walk in the hot sun to get to it. If there is no shade, dig yourself a trench and lie in it. Drape a tarpaulin over the top.

Don't exert yourself physically until nightfall.

Cover your head with a hat or whatever you can.

Do not take all your clothes off. If you have a T-shirt, pee on it then put it on your head. It will cool as the pee evaporates!

RESCUE AND PROTECTION

As in any survival situation, your number one priority is getting rescued.

DO: Use a mirror or a piece of shiny metal to signal for help during the day. Flash it in all directions.

DO: Light a fire at night. It will attract attention from miles around. You can also flash a flashlight on and off.

DO: Try shouting if you see someone in the distance, but don't waste energy. A whistle carries further, or some kind of improvised bell, like a suspended tin can, hit with a knife.

DO: Wear sunglasses or goggles.

DO: Rub soot, boot polish, or burnt cork on your upper cheeks and around your eyes.

DO: Wear a face mask of thin material such as a T-shirt.

FINDING WATER

- Birds circle water holes in true desert areas. In the Sahara, watch for flocks of doves or pigeons.

- Many desert bats visit water at the beginning of their evening flight.

- Animal tracks belonging to a herd are a particularly good sign.

- Places where animals have scratched or where flies hover may show where water lay recently on the surface.

- Water that smells bad is not necessarily unsafe: strain off the algae and bugs (and consider eating them), and purify as usual. (See water filtering on page 33.)

- Desert plants need water to survive. There must be some underneath them.

- Cactuses are best avoided unless you absolutely know what you're doing. The water in them can make you vomit.

Don't be tempted to drink your urine to quench your thirst.

FOOD

FORGET ABOUT IT. PEOPLE DO NOT USUALLY DIE OF STARVATION IN SURVIVAL SITUATIONS. THE HEAT WILL HAVE SAPPED YOUR APPETITE ANYWAY, AND YOUR BODY NEEDS WATER FOR DIGESTION, SO FOOD WILL DEHYDRATE YOU EVEN MORE.

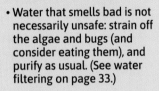

RIVERS AND LAKES

PEOPLE HAVE DROWNED WHEN RESCUING PANICKY SWIMMERS,
SO STAY CALM AND FOLLOW THESE RULES TO SURVIVE FALLING IN.

IF YOU FALL INTO WATER

DO: Try to hold your breath, pinch your nose, and avoid swallowing water.

DO: Try to stand up: many canals, rivers, and ponds are not very deep.

DO: Look for overhanging tree branches or floating debris to cling to.

DO: Tread water if you can't swim. Pedal your legs slowly as if you were cycling, and paddle your hands to add support and balance. Take a couple of big deep breaths to give you buoyancy.

DO: If you can swim, don't waste energy fighting any current. Swim diagonally across it to work your way to a landing point.

DO: Call as loudly as you can for help if you can't swim.

Pedal legs slowly

DON'T: Remove any clothing. Whether you're treading water or swimming, if the water is cold, it'll help keep you warm, and air trapped between clothing layers may also aid buoyancy. Kick off your shoes, though.

DON'T: Panic or struggle. If someone dives in to help you, it probably means they're a strong swimmer and know what they're doing. Relax and let them take charge.

RESCUING SOMEONE FROM WATER

REMEMBER THESE WORDS WHEN RESCUING SOMEONE:
• REACH • THROW • WADE • ROW • REACH

If the person isn't too far away, find something like a stick or branch to **reach** out to them. You can improvise a rope by tying together scarves or pants.

▼

If the person is out of reach, **throw** them a life buoy or anything that floats. If you're throwing a life buoy, throw it underarm and aim it to land beyond the person.

▼

If you're going to **wade** into the water, test the depth with a stick before taking each step forward.

If a dinghy or canoe is nearby and you know how to handle it, you can **row** or paddle out.

▼

If there's no alternative and you are a strong swimmer, swim out to **reach** them with a life buoy or anything buoyant, preferably with a line attached to something or someone on the bank.

SURVIVAL FLOATING

1. BREATHE	2. RELAX	3. FLOAT	4. BREATHE
While floating vertically in the water, take a deep breath.	With your mouth closed, lower your face into the water. Bring your arms forward to rest at surface level.	Float in this position until you need to breathe again.	Treading water, raise your head above the water and breathe out. Take another breath then return to the relaxed position.

 ON THE BEACH

A DAY AT THE BEACH CAN BE VERY RELAXING. BUT PAY ATTENTION TO POTENTIAL HAZARDS IN THE WATER. IT MAY NOT BE AS CALM AS IT APPEARS.

RIP CURRENTS

Rips currents, or rip tides, are powerful currents caused by waves breaking on shallow sandbars and then pushing water back out to sea through deeper channels. People can easily get caught out by rip currents. To an untrained eye, they can look like a good place to enter the water.

TIP

How to spot a rip current:
- Darker patches in the water beside shallower sandbars.
- Rippled or churned water without breaking waves.
- Foam.
- Bits of debris floating out to sea.
- Brown water where the sand has been disturbed.

Rising to tens of yards high, tsunamis are huge waves that strike the coast with devastating force and travel far inland.

As soon as you hear a tsunami alert, evacuate immediately. Use a car, bike, or any available transportation to get away from the coast and head for high ground. Failing that, run as fast as you can, uphill if you can.

ESCAPING RIP CURRENTS

ALERT OTHERS. If you're struggling in a rip current, raise your hand and shout for help.

KEEP HOLD of a bodyboard or surfboard or anything that floats. If you are able to stand, wade out of the current, don't swim. Rips can flow at up to 5 mph (8 km/h), which is faster than an Olympic swimmer!

IN DEEP WATER swim across the direction of the current, parallel to the shore, until you are free. Use any breaking waves to help you get back to the beach.

AVOID THEM! Always swim between the flags and on lifeguarded beaches.

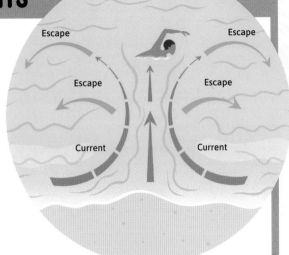

CATCH YOUR BREATH FIRST, then relax and float for around 60–90 seconds. Some rip currents recirculate rather than flow out to sea and may bring you closer to shore.

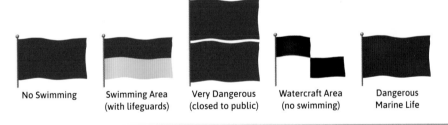

No Swimming	Swimming Area (with lifeguards)	Very Dangerous (closed to public)	Watercraft Area (no swimming)	Dangerous Marine Life

 IF SOMEONE ELSE IS IN TROUBLE

The first challenge is to recognize that they are in difficulty. The signs can easily go unnoticed.

The second challenge is to overcome instinct and selflessness, both of which can spur people to run in to help.

Do NOT enter the water. Focus on fetching help.

SURVIVING AT SEA

AT SEA, YOU SHOULD ONLY ABANDON A LARGER CRAFT FOR A SMALLER ONE IF YOU HAVE TO. BUT YOU MAY BE FORCED TO TAKE TO A LIFE RAFT.

1 BOARDING A LIFE RAFT

DON'T INFLATE A LIFE RAFT until just before you use it. Launch it from the side of the boat away from the wind.

DON'T SWIM unless for a very short distance to the life-raft.

SWIMMERS SHOULD BOARD the life-raft from the upwind side to prevent the bottom of the raft being caught by the wind and tipped.

IF ANYONE IS INJURED, get them to turn their backs to the raft, push them down slightly to benefit from buoyancy when they pop up, then haul them aboard.

ABOARD THE LIFE RAFT

- Move away from a sinking or burning parent craft and post a lookout.
- Bail out any water and collect any survivors.
- Tie the strongest swimmer to the craft with line to stop it from drifting away if it overturns.
- Administer first aid if necessary.
- Prepare all signaling devices for use.
- Collect any useful debris.
- Get everyone to take a seasickness pill.

If there are several rafts, connect them at the lifeline, which encircles the outside of the raft. The line should be about 25 feet (8 m) long.

- Check the craft's general seaworthiness.
- Check that lines are not chafing the craft.
- Check for leaks, and repair them at once.
- Check that others are sleeping safely—not trailing their arms or legs over the side or lying in pools of water.
- Note the craft's direction and speed.

44

EXPOSURE

Do not expose yourself needlessly to the sun and wind. In hot weather, it's better to wear a light layer of clothing than nothing at all. If it's very hot, try dipping your clothes in the sea, wringing them out, then draping them over yourself. The effect of evaporation is cooling.

Use sunscreen from your panic bag on any area of skin that must remain exposed. Wear a hat, preferably one with a brim. Wear sunglasses as the reflection off the water will cause sore eyes.

2 WATER

Don't drink sea water, urine, or human blood. They are so salty that they will take much more water from your system in order to be processed than they put in.

YOUR MARITIME PANIC BAG should contain at least one solar still. Get it going.

USE EVERY MEANS AVAILABLE to catch rainwater: plastic shoes, hats, even cupped hands.

DEW MIGHT FORM on the inside of the raft canopy during the night.

ICEBERGS are a source of fresh water.

3 FOOD

If no water is available, don't eat. If you have ample water, eat whatever protein foods are available first, and save your emergency carbohydrate rations.

Fish juice is not a substitute for water because it contains so much protein, but wet fish is better than dry. And fish eyes contain a lot of water! All sea birds are protein food, as is seaweed—check it for tiny crabs and shrimps.

When fishing remember these rules:
- Never fasten the line to something solid—it may snap in two or damage the life raft if a large fish strikes.
- Fish are more apt to see and strike a moving bait than a still one.
- Don't encourage sharks by trailing your hands or feet in the water.
- Throw waste overboard during the day, when you can watch for sharks.

IN THE TROPICS

YOU'RE PROBABLY SAFER FROM SUDDEN DEATH IN THE JUNGLE THAN IN MOST CITIES. HOWEVER, YOUR RESCUE IS LIKELY TO BE IN YOUR OWN HANDS.

SETTING UP CAMP

Find a stream then follow that until you find a river, then follow that until you find humans... But you may find yourself blocked by vegetation. And you'll need to set up camp.

NIGHT comes very quickly, so prepare early.

LOCATE your shelter away from swamps, on a knoll or high spot in a clearing.

DON'T sleep on the ground. Make a frame of poles, and cover it with palm fronds or other broad leaves. If possible, improvise a hammock.

DO NOT build a shelter under dead trees or under a tree with dead limbs, or under a coconut tree.

DO NOT camp too near a stream or pond, especially during the rainy season.

WATCH OUT FOR INSECTS

The real dangers of the tropics are the insects, many of which pass on diseases and parasites. Smear mud on your face and exposed skin as a protection, especially when sleeping.

Check your body every day for ticks. Burn ticks off with a fire ember, or pull them. The mandibles may be left behind. Treat them as if they were splinters—they are an open invitation to infection.

TRAVEL

- Do not grab at brush or vines when climbing slopes —they may have irritating spines or sharp thorns.
- Avoid obstacles: do not fight them.
- Avoid climbing high terrain, except in order to take your bearings.
- Drink plenty of water, but purify it first.
- Should you contract a fever, make no attempt to travel.

- Protect any wounds by covering them with a clean dressing. Lick even the tiniest of scratches.
- Move carefully through high grass: sharp-edged grasses can cut your clothes to shreds.
- Watch for trees with octopus-like roots and avoid the swamp that they indicate.

CLOTHES

WHEN YOU TAKE YOUR CLOTHES OFF, HANG THEM UP. IF LAID ON THE GROUND THEY MAY COLLECT ANTS, SCORPIONS, OR SNAKES. ALWAYS CHECK FOOTWEAR AND CLOTHING BEFORE PUTTING THEM ON.

FOOD AND WATER

Food and water are normally plentiful, but purify water first. Animal trails often lead to water. Coconuts (especially green, unripe ones) contain drinkable liquid. But don't drink just coconut water or you'll get the runs!

Do not drink any fluid that looks milky, except in a coconut. Water can be obtained from muddy streams or lakes by digging a hole on the land about 3 feet (1 m) from the bank. Allow the water to seep in and the mud to settle.

Water can be obtained from vines. Cut a deep notch in the vine as high up as you can reach. Cut the vine off close to the ground and let the water drip into your mouth or a container. When the water stops dripping, cut another deep notch below the first. Repeat until the supply of water is exhausted.

Bamboo stems often have water in the hollow joints. Shake the stems of old, yellowish bamboo. If you hear a gurgling sound, cut a notch at the base of each joint and catch the water in a container.

Watch the monkeys. Anything they eat, so can you!

RAPID ACTIONS

REMEMBER, YOU ARE NOT A CASUALTY, YOU'RE A SURVIVOR! THERE IS A SIMPLE DRILL THAT CAN SAVE YOU IN JUST ABOUT EVERY SITUATION.

TOP PRIORITIES

AWAY FROM DANGER: Move yourself and others away from any further danger.

FIRST AID: Check yourself and others for injuries and apply first aid if necessary.

STORES: If it's safe to do so, move any stores that might come in handy away from danger.

RESCUE SIGNALS

RESCUERS WILL BE TRYING TO FIND YOU QUICKLY, SO YOU MUST START THINKING ABOUT ATTRACTING ATTENTION TO YOURSELF AS SOON AS YOU CAN.

SOS

The three-letter code **SOS** is an internationally recognized distress signal. In Morse code, it consists of three short dots, three long dashes, and three short dots—but any signal repeated three times will do.

SOUND SIGNALS

If you have a whistle, use three short blasts, three long ones, then three short ones.

SIGNAL FIRE

You'll need lots of smoke during daylight, lots of flame at night. For smoke, burn a vehicle tire or plastic, or pile green leaves onto to your fire when you hear planes or other signs of rescuers.

SIGHT SIGNALS

Mirror flashes can be seen up to 25 miles (40 km) away. Improvise your own with a laminated ID card, a shard of glass, a CD, or the glass face of a cell phone.

SHOULD I STAY OR SHOULD I GO?

SURVIVORS HAVE A STRONG URGE TO MOVE. EXPERTS CALL THIS "GET HOME-ITIS," BUT IF YOU POSSIBLY CAN, IT IS BEST TO STAY PUT.

REASONS FOR STAYING

People will come looking for a missing aircraft, boat, or car, and will be looking for the vehicle, not the occupants.

▼

A vehicle is much larger than a person, and therefore easier to spot.

▼

Wreckage can provide shelter against wind, wet, heat, and moderate cold.

▼

Materials for making distress signals are more readily available from a wrecked or stranded vehicle.

▼

A vehicle, particularly an aircraft, might be carrying water, food, and first aid supplies, as well as clothing.

▼

Traveling may well be so dangerous that it should only be undertaken when there is absolutely no chance of rescue.

REASONS FOR GOING

You know you will not be missed for a long time.

▼

The place where you are stranded makes it unlikely that you will be spotted—for example, a jungle or dense forest.

▼

There has been no sign of a search party after several days.

▼

Search aircraft or search-parties have been spotted, but they have not responded to your distress signals.

▼

To stay with the wreckage might be more dangerous than to leave it—you might be at high altitude, or in a precarious position.

SECONDARY ACTIONS

IF YOU ARE AWAY FROM DANGER, THERE ARE FOUR MORE IMMEDIATE THREATS: PANIC, EXTREME COLD, EXTREME HEAT, AND LACK OF WATER.

KEEP CALM

TAKE A DEEP BREATH:
Keep calm. It is hardest to follow procedures during the first 30 seconds after an emergency. Stay calm for this 30 seconds, and your chances of survival are much increased.

TAKE STOCK:
Make a list of stores, materials, and everyone's skills.

LOCATION:
Where are you? How can you help others find you? Prepare signals. Make decisions about staying put or traveling.

Survival is all about staying alive until you are rescued. Keeping a calm head is crucial to your chances.

WATER:
Without water, survival is measured in days.

FOOD:
Without food, survival is measured in weeks—but your body will be going steadily downhill.

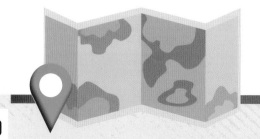

DON'T FORGET YOUR MENTAL HEALTH

AFTER A DISASTER, YOU MAY BE COLD, HUNGRY, THIRSTY, LONELY, IN PAIN, EXHAUSTED, OR BEREAVED, AND ANY ONE OF THESE CAN BE ENOUGH TO ENDANGER YOUR SURVIVAL.

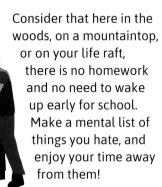

Do anything, to make yourself feel better. Build a shelter. Light a fire. Organize a means of signaling. Sing. Eat your last candy. Anything. The longer you do nothing, the worse you'll feel.

Consider that here in the woods, on a mountaintop, or on your life raft, there is no homework and no need to wake up early for school. Make a mental list of things you hate, and enjoy your time away from them!

Consider how well adapted humans are to the situation you're in. You can eat anything that a rat can eat and more. Humans can survive very well on an all-meat diet, a vegetarian diet or, for quite a few days, nothing at all. You'll be OK!

TRUE STORY

In 2012, eight-year-old Johaven Gonzales and his family were almost killed when their car fell off the side of a mountain in Arizona. Johaven called the emergency services on his sister's mobile phone, but instead of waiting for them to arrive he climbed out of the wrecked vehicle and climbed the 100-foot (30-m) cliff to seek help. Police officers said that had Johaven not climbed the mountain, his family would have died.

PROTECTING YOUR MIND

DON'T PANIC! STAY CALM AND MAKE A PLAN.
REMEMBER: YOU'LL SURVIVE IF YOU THINK YOU CAN.

SIT DOWN!

Once you are out of immediate danger, that is the time to sit down and make a plan.

THE MOMENT you have carried out the immediate action drills and taken shelter, sit down.

IT'S VERY DIFFICULT to panic when you're sitting down.

IF YOUR ONLY PROBLEM is that you are lost, sit down.

IF YOU'RE SITTING DOWN, you present less body area to the elements and so the risk of hypothermia is reduced. You use less precious energy.

JUST BY BEING in a seated position, you'll feel more relaxed and soothed, and able to think more clearly.

CALM DOWN

While you're sitting down, look around you. Try to feel the serenity and beauty of the landscape. Breathe gently and with control. As you breathe out, say aloud: "Calm..." Keep doing it until you are calm.

▼

Think of a time or a place where you have been warm and contented. Relax with this image, instructing each part of your body to respond to it now as it did then. Imagine the tension and anxiety floating away. Gradually breathe more deeply, and each time you breathe out, say: "Calm ..."

▼

Now think. Be prepared to take responsibility for what happens to you, including your inner feelings. Your survival is in your hands. Make some positive statements to yourself, such as: "I know I can make it," or "This situation will not frighten me." If you prefer, you can make a strongly negative 'positive' statement, such as "They will not get at me."

EVALUATE

The time to evaluate is when you've got your feet up relaxing. Easily, calmly, systematically, weigh the situation up. Is anybody injured? How extensive are their injuries? Will people come looking for you? What's the weather like? What's the terrain like? What is available to make your life more comfortable?

USEFUL ITEMS

ORDINARY ITEMS CAN HAVE MANY USES.

Keys can become fishing lures. Sharpened by rubbing on a rough stone surface, they can also be used as cutting tools or scrapers.

Key rings can provide the wire or metal parts for trap triggers, snares or holders for cooking utensils.

Coins can be sharpened and used as cutters. Small ones can become fishing lures.

Lipstick can be used to prevent chapped lips or as a sunburn preventive, or even as a soothing treatment for minor scratches and abrasions. It can also be used as a direction marker, or for writing messages.

Combs are an excellent morale booster—there's nothing like tidy hair for making you feel good (apart from brushing your teeth). The teeth of steel combs can be sharpened, broken off, and used as sewing needles.

Material such as clothing, if it's not needed for anything else, can be unraveled for thread. Webbing belts can be unraveled to produce yards of strong cord.

Belt buckles can become tools. Leather belts can be cut to produce yards of leather thong.

WILD ANIMALS

SOME ANIMALS ARE LESS DANGEROUS THAN YOU MIGHT THINK. OTHERS MAY BE SURPRISINGLY DEADLY. HERE ARE SOME LIFE-SAVING TIPS.

CROCS

Crocodiles and alligators are some of the most fearsome predators on Earth. Crocodiles tend to live in saltwater habitats such as mangrove swamps, while alligators hang out in freshwater marshes and lakes. Both like slow-moving water.

DO: Stay away from the water's edge, especially at night.

DO: Hit it in the eyes or on the nose with a stick or any weapon you have.

DO: Outrun a crocodile by running in a straight line, and fast!

DO: Try to get on the crocodile's back and push down on its neck, if one goes for you on land.

DO: Jam your fingers into its nose if it has you in its jaws.

DON'T: Create splashes or shout if you see a crocodile while swimming. Be as quiet as you can and swim away slowly.

DON'T: Approach a crocodile if you see one on land. Stand still, then back away slowly.

DON'T: Struggle or thrash if it's got you in a "death roll." Roll with it so your arms and legs don't get ripped out of their sockets.

DON'T: Lose hope. The moment you feel its jaws loosen, pull away quickly before it bites again.

KILLER BEASTS

WOLVES KILL **10 PEOPLE** A YEAR.

LIONS KILL **20 PEOPLE** A YEAR.

SHARKS KILL **100 PEOPLE** A YEAR.

ELEPHANTS AND HIPPOS KILL MORE THAN **500 PEOPLE** A YEAR.

CROCODILES ACCOUNT FOR **1,000 DEATHS** A YEAR.

SNAKE BITES KILL **100,000 PEOPLE** A YEAR.

TRUE STORY

In 2017, 10-year-old Juliana Ossa was sitting in shallow water near the shore of a lake in Florida when an alligator lunged out of the water and clamped its jaws onto her leg. Juliana remembered a lifesaving trick she had learned. Jamming her fingers into the animal's nose, she forced it to open its mouth to breathe. The second the alligator let go of her leg, Juliana was up and running. Her family took her to the hospital, where she made a full recovery.

JELLYFISH

Jellyfish are sea creatures with a nearly transparent body and tentacles that can leave you in a world of pain—or even kill you. Each tentacle is covered in thousands of tiny spears packed with venom and triggered by touch.

Some jellyfish are more dangerous than others. The irukandji jellyfish (bottom left) is smaller than a fingernail, but its sting could kill you.

WHAT TO DO

IF YOU'VE BEEN STUNG
• DON'T PANIC • KEEP CALM • BREATHE SLOWLY

Get yourself or the victim out of the water, taking care you are not stung even more.

▼

Don't scratch the sting site—it will only spread the venom and worsen the stinging sensation. Do not pee on it.

▼

Use tweezers to remove any tentacles stuck to the victim's body, or use a credit card, seashell, even a magazine to gently scrape over the affected area and remove any stings on the skin. Wear gloves to do this.

▼

Then you just have to wait it out, though you can also apply a cream containing a painkiller or antihistamine.

SNAKES

Most snakes are neither dangerous nor venomous, yet they kill 100,000 people a year worldwide. Most bites occur when people are trying to catch snakes.

DO: Stand very still. Snakes can strike over half their body length in the blink of an eye.

DO: Stop walking if the snake is following you. The vibration of your feet might have confused it.

DO: Stay calm if bitten. You need a slow heart rate to slow the spread of venom.

DO: Wash the bite with soap and water. Keep it immobilized in a position lower than the heart to slow the flow of poison.

DO: Wrap a bandage tightly above the wound to stop the spread of venom.

DON'T: Make it feel cornered. Back away very slowly, giving it lots of room.

DON'T: Suck out the venom if bitten. The same goes for applying something cold or hot on the wound. You'll just make things worse.

BEAR ATTACKS

BEARS USUALLY AVOID CONTACT WITH HUMANS IF THEY CAN, BUT IF THEY FEEL THREATENED OR CORNERED, THEY MAY ATTACK. HERE'S WHAT TO DO.

AVOID BEARS ENTIRELY

LEAVE THEIR FOOD ALONE. Stay away from any dead animals you come across.

▼

TRAVEL IN GROUPS. Bears will avoid groups of smelly humans.

▼

BE NOISY. If a bear hears you coming, it will try to avoid you.

IF A BEAR NOTICES YOU...

DO: Stay calm. Remember that most bears don't want to attack.

DO: Talk calmly so that the bear knows you are not a prey animal.

DO: Move away slowly and sideways if the bear is still.

DO: Leave the bear an escape route.

DON'T: Make any loud noises.

DON'T: Run. A bear can outrun a human.

DON'T: Climb a tree. Bears can also climb trees.

DON'T: Give the bear your food.

KNOW YOUR BEARS

DESPITE THEIR NAME, NOT ALL AMERICAN BLACK BEARS ARE BLACK. LEARN THE DIFFERENCES AND KNOW WHAT BEAR YOU ARE FACED WITH.

BROWN/GRIZZLY BEARS

- Stand 3–5 feet (1–1.5 m) at the shoulders
- Shoulder hump
- Rump lower than shoulders
- Dish-shaped face from the muzzle to the eyes
- Short, round ears
- Long, slightly rounded claws

AMERICAN BLACK BEARS

- Stand 2–3.5 feet (0.6–1 m) at the shoulders
- No shoulder hump
- Rump higher than shoulders
- Straight face from the muzzle to the eyes
- Tall, prominent ears
- Shorter, curved claws

IF YOU ARE ATTACKED…

YOUR RESPONSE TO A BEAR ATTACK WILL DEPEND ON WHAT KIND OF BEAR IT IS.

BROWN/GRIZZLY BEARS:
Fighting back usually makes things worse. Lay flat on your stomach with your hands behind your neck, spread your legs, and PLAY DEAD. Only fight back if the attack persists.

BLACK BEARS:
Playing dead won't work with black bears. You must either try to escape or fight back. Use whatever you have to hand to hit the bear in the face.

If any bear attacks you in your tent, you must fight back. The bear is probably looking for food and may see you as potential prey.

ANDY SAYS

If you are traveling through bear country, carry bear pepper spray. It can stop a charging bear in its tracks.

BEES

ONE OR TWO STINGS ARE NOT TOO DANGEROUS, UNLESS YOU ARE ALLERGIC. BUT IF A WHOLE SWARM OF BEES STINGS YOU, IT'S A DIFFERENT MATTER.

BEE WARE

DON'T SWAT or try to hurt bees. They can send "help" signals that can travel amazing distances.

IF A BEE is constantly bumping into you, this can mean it thinks you're threatening its hive, and is calling for backup. A swarm could attack soon, so move away quickly.

IF A SWARM appears, you MUST run to shelter. Run in a straight line. You can outrun a swarm, but run as fast as you can.

PROTECT YOUR HEAD! As you run, pull your shirt over your head to protect your ears, nose, mouth, and eyes. If you can't do that, use your hands to protect your face.

FIND THE SHELTER of a building or vehicle—anywhere with a door.

IF ESCAPE ISN'T possible and you are wearing a dark-colored top, take it off and flail it around. The bees might see it as an enemy animal and back off.

ONCE YOU ARE SAFE

1. Get any stings out as soon as you can. Never try to squeeze stings out with your fingers or tweezers. Instead, scrape the stings out using your fingernails or a credit card, magazine, or any other flat, straight-edged surface.

2. When the stings are out, clean the welts with soap and water.

3. If you feel sick after being stung, have trouble breathing, experience severe swelling, or exhibit other signs of an allergic reaction, GET IMMEDIATE MEDICAL HELP.

ELEPHANT ATTACKS

Elephant attacks are responsible for hundreds of deaths a year. If you are out on a safari, you need to know how to deal with an aggressive elephant.

Elephants are highly intelligent and generally peaceful animals. Sadly, they are poached for their tusks. In areas where elephants are heavily poached, they have learned that people can be their enemies and are much more likely to attack.

If you see a herd of elephants:
1. Keep your distance.
2. Do not sneak up on the herd.
3. Stay well away from baby elephants. The adults fiercely protect their young.
4. Big bulls in "musth" are particularly dangerous. These are males who are looking to mate and can be very aggressive. Try to avoid them.

ELEPHANT CHARGES

BLUFF CHARGE

An elephant will use a bluff charge to intimidate you. It will spread its ears wide and sway from side to side. If an elephant bluff charges you, stay calm and talk in a soft voice. With luck, the elephant will calm down when it realizes that you are not a threat.

ATTACK CHARGE

If an elephant really means business, it will pin its ears back on its head. At this point, you need to RUN. Run in a zig-zag and try to get a big object between you and the elephant.

TIP Elephants are scared of bees. Studies have shown that African elephants will back down when played the sound of African bees. They really hate being stung!

STORMS

MANY STORMS CARRY THE THREAT OF LIGHTNING, WHILE THE EXTREME WINDS OF A HURRICANE CAN FLATTEN BUILDINGS.

LIGHTNING

If your skin starts to tingle, you have a metallic taste in your mouth, or if the hairs on your arms start to rise, that's a sure sign of electricity in the air.

COUNT THE SECONDS between seeing the lightning and hearing the next thunderclap. If it's less than 30 seconds, get inside.

SPREAD OUT if you're in a group.

A SOLID BUILDING is the best place to shelter, but not isolated barns and huts. Next best place to shelter is a car. Make sure the windows are closed and don't touch anything metal inside.

AVOID:

Gazebos, the shelter of tree branches, or anything that's not enclosed.

Open areas, especially hills.

Metal objects like golf clubs, ski poles, or fences.

Pools, rivers, or lakes.

Cave entrances or other overhangs. A deep cave is safe—go to the back.

Lightning finds the nearest way to the ground, so if you find yourself in the middle of a field, don't try to run. Drop to your knees and bend over.

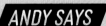
ANDY SAYS

When Thunder Roars, Go Indoors! Lightning is one of the biggest weather-related causes of death and injury worldwide.

EARTHQUAKE!

Earthquakes are devastating natural disasters that can destroy entire communities. There's no accurate way of predicting them.

SURVIVING AN EARTHQUAKE

IF YOU'RE INDOORS

If you're in a building, stay calm and try to reassure others. Never leave the building during an earthquake. If you're near any tall shelves, televisions, or glass windows, you'll need to move away immediately.

Drop onto your hands and knees right where you are.

Cover your head and neck with anything at hand—your arms if nothing else. Then get under something solid and sturdy, such as a desk or table.

Hold on like this until the shaking stops.

IF YOU'RE OUTDOORS

If you can do so safely, get to a clear area away from tall buildings, power lines, and trees. You don't want any of that stuff falling on you.

IF YOU'RE IN A VEHICLE

Stop the car and stay in it. Crouch below the level of the seats, and cover your head and neck with your hands.

IF YOU'RE ON THE BEACH

An earthquake can trigger a tsunami. Move to higher ground.

IF YOU'RE IN A WHEELCHAIR

Look around for shelter and try to get there as fast as you can. Then lock your wheels and cover your head and neck with your hands.

IF YOU'RE IN A STADIUM

Stay where you are. Get on the floor in the space in front of your seat, bend over, and cover your head and neck with your hands. Stay calm.

EVACUATE!

If you are advised to evacuate the area, make sure your family does so. Head for high ground—as high above any possible flood level as you can. If your family has a car, it should have been topped up with fuel when the warnings began. Your parents should drive everyone out of the danger area when told to do so.

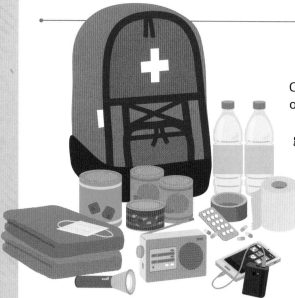

BE PREPARED!

Lock doors and windows securely. Close any window shutters. Put strips of duct tape across windows in a star pattern to reduce the risk of flying glass if the wind shatters the panes. Keep well away from all windows. Each family member should have prepared an emergency bag, or grab bag (see page 108).

TIP Shortly after the worst of the storm, there may be a period of calm. This occurs as the "eye" of the hurricane passes overhead. Beware! In less than an hour, the winds will pick up again.

CAUGHT OUT IN THE OPEN

If you are caught out in the open, lie flat on the ground. Crawl on your stomach to the sheltered side of anything that will break the full force of the wind—a large boulder, a belt of trees, an outcrop of rock. If you are close to trees, however, watch out for falling branches or even trees themselves if they've been uprooted.

TORNADO!

Tornadoes, also known as "twisters," are the world's most violent winds. They can be even more destructive than hurricanes.

OFTEN YOU WILL HEAR a

tornado before you see it. Listen out for a sound like a waterfall that turns into a roar like a huge jet engine as it gets closer. The sky often turns dark with a green tinge just before a storm hits, and it may suddenly start to hail. Another sign might be debris, such as dust, branches, and leaves, dropping from the sky. You may notice clouds that are moving very fast, perhaps twisting into a cone shape. When the tornado arrives, you can expect to see a funnel-shaped cloud that is spinning rapidly. Debris will be pulled upward into the vortex like a giant vacuum cleaner.

GET INSIDE! The best place to be when a tornado arrives is inside, and preferably in a specially built storm cellar.

IN A CAR, if you have enough warning, the best way to avoid a tornado is to figure out the direction it's going and drive at 90 degrees from this direction.

STUCK OUTSIDE, if the only shelter you can find is in a ditch or hollow, make sure you lie face down and use your arms to protect your head and neck.

AVALANCHE

HUNDREDS OF PEOPLE DIE IN AVALANCHES EACH YEAR, BUT MANY OF THEM MIGHT HAVE SAVED THEMSELVES IF ONLY THEY'D KNOWN WHAT TO DO.

AVOID!

PREVENTION IS BETTER than cure. The best way to avoid getting caught in an avalanche is to steer clear of places where avalanches happen.

CHECK WITH LOCALS if you can, and always follow their warnings. Don't ski or hike alone. Steer clear of snow-capped mountains with steep slopes between 30–45 degrees. Walk or ski along ridges, and not down snowy valleys without trees.

An avalanche is a mass of snow and ice that suddenly slides down a mountain, carrying rocks with it.

MANY AVALANCHES are caused by the movement of people. If you're with a group, space yourselves out.

ACT FAST! Usually, avalanches start slowly, and then accelerate. If an avalanche is rushing toward you, try to get above it by moving up to a ridge. If that's not possible, seek shelter behind the biggest tree in sight.

IF YOU ARE CAUGHT, keep your head up and swim. Backstroke is best so your face is pointing up, but don't worry about style. Thrashing, kicking, breaststroke, whatever keeps you near the surface. There's a good chance that you could swim right to the surface, and being stuck in this position after an avalanche is better than being stuck under snow.

STUCK UNDER SNOW

THIS ISN'T LIKE THE FLUFFY STUFF YOU'RE USED TO. ONCE IT STOPS, THE SNOW WILL FEEL JUST LIKE WET CONCRETE. IT WILL BE PITCH BLACK AND YOUR AIR SUPPLY IS GOING TO BE LIMITED.

First, get your hands in front of your face to create an air pocket—the bigger the better. Try rotating your head to make the air pocket bigger.

▼

Stay calm. The slower your breathing is, the longer your air supply is going to last.

▼

If you can dig, you will need to determine which way is up. To do this, let spit dribble from your mouth. Gravity will take it down. Your biggest concern now is breathing, and this won't be easy.

✚ KEEP BREATHING ✚

To make matters even worse, your warm breath can melt the snow in front of your face. That water will likely re-freeze into ice, and you're left with a layer of ice that seals you in with the CO_2 you're exhaling. To avoid suffocating, punch your hand to the surface. If you can wiggle it around, this creates an air shaft. It also offers a clear signal to rescuers. You have the best chance of survival if you're rescued within the first 15 minutes. You need to draw attention to yourself.

⊕ FIRST AID

THIS SECTION GIVES A BASIC LIST OF MEDICAL EMERGENCIES AND THEIR TREATMENTS. WITH LUCK YOU'LL NEVER HAVE TO USE THEM, BUT EMERGENCY FIRST-AID SKILLS COULD SAVE YOUR LIFE OR THE LIVES OF OTHERS.

TAKE A COURSE

There's really no way to learn and practice all these critical skills just by reading a chapter in a book. Take a first-aid course to get the experience that you need to be properly prepared. Ask your teacher if the school could organize a first aid course for your grade level.

There will be two major differences between what you will learn in your first-aid course and the sort of emergency measures you will need to apply in a survival situation.

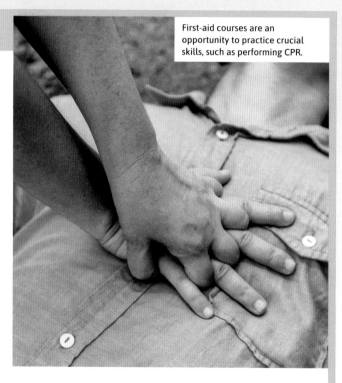

First-aid courses are an opportunity to practice crucial skills, such as performing CPR.

In the normal world, first aid is usually about short-term treatment to stabilize an injury until an ambulance arrives. Under survival conditions, you may have to use the injured part of your body to deal with higher priorities, such as shelter-building or signaling. When that happens, you'll have to bite the bullet and get on with it.

The most important skill, as ever, is the ability to stay calm so you can assess the situation rationally, make a plan, and deal with the circumstances.

"DR ABC"

USE THIS PRIMARY SURVEY TO
QUICKLY ASSESS THE CASUALTY.

1. DANGER: Before approaching the casualty, always make sure the area is safe.

▼

2. RESPONSE: Ask questions to see if you can get a response. Kneel next to their chest and gently shake their shoulders, asking, "What has happened?', 'Open your eyes!" If the casualty does not respond, they should be treated urgently.

▼

3. AIRWAY: Open the airway by placing one hand on the forehead to tilt the head back and using two fingers from the other hand to lift the chin.

▼

4. BREATHING: Place your ear above the casualty's mouth. Listen for sounds of breathing and see if you can feel their breath. Watch to see if their chest moves. Do this for 10 seconds. If they are not breathing, you need to start CPR immediately—see right.

▼

5. CIRCULATION: If they are breathing, check for signs of severe bleeding.

PERFORMING CPR

CPR is an emergency procedure performed on people experiencing cardiac arrest. Its primary purpose is to provide oxygen to the brain, and to continue it until the patient's heartbeat can be restored.

START PUMPING

Roll the person onto their back and begin chest compressions immediately. Place the heel of one hand on the center of the victim's chest and put your other hand over the top of it, interlacing your fingers. You want to compress the chest about 2 inches (5 cm) deep, 30 times. Don't worry about hurting them—even if you break some ribs, you're saving their life.

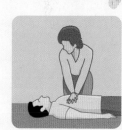

KEEP GOING!

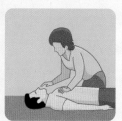

Keep your arms straight and pump hard and fast, at a rate of about 100 compressions per minute. If you know the song *Stayin' Alive* by the Bee Gees, that's a good reminder of the beat to follow. Keep going for as long as you can. If there is someone to help you, take turns. If they are responsive and breathing move on to circulation.

SEVERE BLEEDING

WITH A HEAVILY BLEEDING WOUND, THE MOST IMPORTANT CONCERN IS TO STEM THE BLEEDING AS SOON AS POSSIBLE.

WIPE THE WOUND thoroughly and try to spot the bleeding points. Try direct pressure on these points and bind up the wound. If the dressing doesn't soak itself with blood, leave it for twenty-four hours, then tease out the packing and expose the wound to nature's finest healing agent: the air.

IF IT'S STILL BLEEDING, try the process again. Still blood everywhere? Pinch each bleeding point and tie it off. Do not stitch the wound.

IF YOU'RE STILL HAVING TROUBLE, locate the nearest artery. Place pressure on it with your fingers while keeping pressure on the wound with the other hand. Pressure points for your arm are just above the elbow and just below the inside of your armpit; in your leg, the pressure points are in the groin and behind the knee.

FOR A MAJOR CUT on your arm, hand, foot, or leg, you should hold whatever body part it is above the level of your heart. This will make it much harder for the blood to flow, which makes the bleeding slow.

FRACTURES

Assuming there's no hope of rescue within the next few days, simple fractures must be set.

First, compare the damaged limb with the undamaged one, to make sure it is fractured. If you think it is, immobilize it with two splints so it doesn't move around and do more damage.

If there are no splints in your first-aid kit, you can improvise one with sticks. Pad the area with clothing, then immobilize with the sticks and wrap tightly.

DRESSING THE WOUND

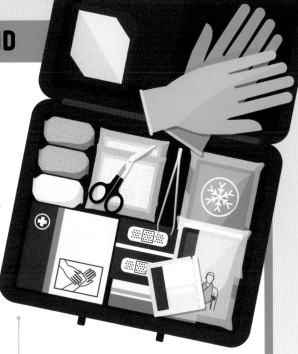

Once the bleeding has stopped, inspect the rest of the wound and clean it if necessary. Dead tissue and any pieces of fat present should be cut away, and foreign bodies picked out carefully. (Live tissue bleeds gently; dead tissue doesn't.)

If you don't have a first-aid kit with gauze or wound padding, use items of clothing. Apply pressure directly to the wound site to stop the bleeding and hold pressure on there for about twenty minutes without lifting up to see if the bleeding is stopped. Use your bare hands if necessary.

Don't remove the gauze or clothing if it gets soaked through with blood. Add more on top and continue to put pressure on the wound.

Never sew up a wound. It must be allowed to heal from the inside outward. Leave it open to the air and bear in mind that sunlight destroys bacteria. Even deep, penetrating wounds should be opened right up and allowed to heal from the inside outward.

TIP

Never pull out an impaled object—it will only cause the wound to bleed faster. Instead, leave the object in place and dress the area around the wound.

SPRAINS

A sprain can be as painful and incapacitating as a break. Follow the rules of RICE.

REST as much as possible for the first two days. Avoid putting weight on the affected area as this is likely to cause more damage and delay recovery.

ICE the injury for about 20 minutes every few hours. Use an ice pack covered in a light towel. A bag of frozen peas will also work.

COMPRESS the injured area by wrapping it with an elastic medical bandage. This will prevent swelling.

ELEVATE the injured body part above the level of your heart. This reduces pain, throbbing, and swelling.

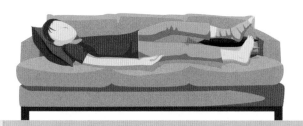

If you have them, use anti-inflammatory medications to reduce the swelling and ease the pain. After a few icing cycles, you may be OK to walk.

TREATING SHOCK

Shock is a condition that can accompany trauma, blood loss, heat stroke, an allergic reaction, and other ailments. It can lead to organ damage and death.

SYMPTOMS:
- Cool and clammy skin
- Low blood pressure
- Weak and rapid pulse
- Shallow rapid breathing
- Weak with vacant eyes
- Confusion
- Nausea

WHAT TO DO:
- Lay the victim down and lift their feet about 1 foot (30 cm) off the ground—unless their head, neck, back, or legs are injured.
- Check for breathing and begin CPR if necessary.
- If the victim is vomiting or bleeding from their mouth, roll them on their side to prevent choking.
- Keep them warm by covering them with a sleeping bag and removing any restrictive clothing.
- Don't give the victim anything to eat or drink.

MINOR INJURIES

SPLINTERS

If you find any splinters, try placing the affected area of skin in firm contact with the top of a bottle or jar partly filled with hot water. The exposed flesh will be sucked into the top of the container, which may start the splinter moving. If that doesn't work, remove the splinter by any means you can. Enlarge the wound so that it can heal from the inside outward. Now keep the cleaned wound exposed to the air.

CUTS

Apply pressure to the area for about 10 minutes, which should be enough to help stop the bleeding. Use butterfly bandages to close any large cuts and cover the wound with a gauze pad.

BLISTERS

Try to keep blisters from popping for as long as possible. The skin under the blister is raw and healing.

BURNS

For small burns, immediately put the limb in cold water or cover it with a water-soaked bandana. Keep it cool, then cover it with a gauze pad. For large burns, don't immerse the burn site in water because that can cause shock. Cover a large burn with clingfilm if you have any, or a cool moist bandage, lift the site above heart level if that's possible, then get the victim to a hospital as fast as you can. Do not pull off any clothing.

Splinter

Blister

Minor burn

FROSTBITE

Frostbite can occur at any time in cold weather. Wind chill factor is important here, because wind lowers the temperature dramatically. At very low temperatures, your flesh can freeze in under 60 seconds. Any exposed part of the body—usually the fingers, nose, ears, and toes—can easily become frostbitten. There are three degrees of frostbite.

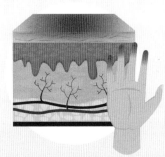  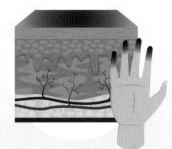

FIRST DEGREE: The flesh is white or blue, waxy/frosty-looking and fairly pliable. Fingers are stiff and numb. After re-warming, the skin may peel or blister.

SECOND DEGREE: The flesh is rather mushy, like semi-frozen ice cream. When thawed, it blisters and may turn black. The skin may peel off.

THIRD DEGREE: Frozen solid. Be careful as the frozen parts are brittle and can snap off. When thawed, the skin blisters badly. The victim may well lose the damaged part.

✚ TREATMENT ✚

Discover frostbite quickly before there is much chance of damage. Check for it every three to five minutes by wiggling your toes and crinkling up your face. If any area is numb, thaw it and protect from further frostbite by covering it up.

The best way to thaw minor frostbite is in warm water. But you must be in a place where your entire body can stay warm before the thawing process is started. If you are cold, there will not be enough blood to the damaged area after it has thawed. Continue thawing for at least 30 minutes. This will be painful!

If no warm water is available, use armpits, stomach, or crotch as a heat source. Fire is dangerous as the frozen area will be so numb that it could be burned before the victim realizes.

After thawing, bandage the affected area loosely.

Third degree frostbite should not be treated unless you are sure that rescue is more than a few days away,. You can walk on frozen feet for a whole day without causing any further damage.

SNOW OR SUN BLINDNESS

The symptoms of snow and sun blindness are the same. Your eyes will begin to feel as though they are full of sand and start to burn. Suddenly things become hazy.

THE PAIN INCREASES horrendously until finally you can no longer see. Blindness will start a few hours after exposure and last a few days. Prevention is definitely better than cure! If you don't have protective sunglasses or goggles, you must improvise some at once.

USE A HANDKERCHIEF, bandana, scarf, or some article of clothing, tied over your face, with tiny slits for each eye. Or use adhesive tape or mud, even blood, over your regular eyeglasses, so that just a small peep-hole is left through each lens.

TREATMENT

Put a bandage over both eyes to block out all light absolutely. Any light at all will aggravate the burning and watering of your inflamed eyes and also cause headaches and bad vision. You will now be incapacitated for up to a week.

FIRST-AID KITS

Besides a first-aid kit, you'll find duct tape is a great thing to carry. If you're on a hiking trip, just wind a big length of it around your water bottle so it doesn't take up any room.

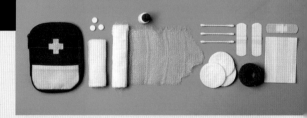

In an emergency, duct tape can be used on blisters and to cover wounds. Not perfect, but it gets the job done. Also in an emergency, superglue works well with cuts and other wounds. Simply pinch the wound closed and apply superglue to the surrounding skin. This is perfectly safe and will do a great job of holding the wound shut until you find medical help.

> ## ANDY SAYS
> **Pain can be one of the biggest enemies to survival.** Tell the affected part to stop bothering you: if it wants to hurt, that is its business and nothing to do with you.

QUIZ

1 WHEN USING A WATCH TO FIND YOUR DIRECTION, DO YOU POINT THE HOUR AT:

A. The sun

B. The moon

C. The ground

2 HOW DO YOU IMPROVE A COMPASS NEEDLE'S EFFICIENCY?

A. Wind it with cotton thread

B. Bend it 180 degrees

C. Stroke it with a magnet

3 TO AVOID HEATSTROKE, YOU SHOULD IMMEDIATELY:

A. Undress

B. Get out of the sun

C. Eat something spicy

4 YOU SHOULDN'T EAT BRIGHTLY COLORED INSECTS, BECAUSE…

A. They might bite you

B. They are probably toxic

C. They will be able to fly away quickly

5 WHICH OF THESE MAKES GREAT EMERGENCY FUEL FOR A FIRE?

A. Oranges

B. Tomato soup

C. Corn chips

6 WHAT BODILY SUBSTANCE CAN YOU USE TO TEST THE FRESHNESS OF WATER?

A. Boogers

B. Earwax

C. Belly button fluff

7 TSUNAMIS ARE:

A. Dangerous earthquakes

B. Gigantic underground chasms

C. Huge waves that strike the coast

8 WHICH OF THESE WILL HELP IF YOU'RE BITTEN BY A CROCODILE?

A. Singing it to sleep

B. Jamming your fingers in its nose

C. Swimming deep underwater

9 'WHEN THUNDER ROARS, GO...'

A. Indoors

B. Fishing

C. Crazy

10 WHICH OF THESE ANIMALS IS RESPONSIBLE FOR THE MOST DEATHS PER YEAR?

A. Sharks

B. Lions

C. Crocodiles

Answers on page 143

SURVIVING IN THE CITY

THE IMPORTANT SURVIVAL SKILLS

THE MOST EFFECTIVE SURVIVAL SKILLS ARE OFTEN THE SIMPLEST. IF YOU FIND YOURSELF IN TROUBLE, YOU NEED TO KNOW HOW TO GET HELP.

1 CALLING THE EMERGENCY SERVICES

The most important survival skill is in knowing know how to call the emergency services in your own country or a country that you're visiting.

▼

If you're at home and have Alexa, Siri, or Google Assistant, you can ask them to call.

▼

If you're calling an emergency service, always give them your address first. Only after that should you explain the reason for your call. That way, even if something or somebody forces you to end the conversation, the operator will already know where to send help.

▼

Don't know where you are? If you have a mobile phone and the What3Words app, it will give you a three-word phrase that you can give the operator. What3Words assigns each 10-foot square on Earth its own combination of three words.

▼

If you don't have a mobile phone, tell the operator any landmarks you can see.

2 HAVE A FAMILY CODE WORD

The next most important survival skill is that your family should have a code word that can be used in many situations.

▼

If anyone ever approaches you claiming your parents sent them to collect you, they must know the code word. If they don't know the code word, you don't go with them.

▼

If the stranger does not know the code word, you should move away immediately and look for help.

▼

If you are at a friend's house and something makes you feel unsafe, call your parents and use the code word.

▼

If you are in public and you spot a safety threat, you can use the code word to warn your family to exit quickly or take shelter.

HELP SIGNAL

WHAT TO DO

If you can't speak or shout to tell people you need help, learn this new signal that went viral on TikTok. To do the hand gesture, follow these steps.

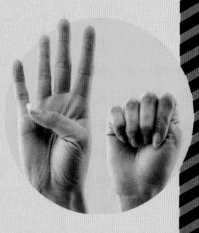

- Hold up your palm
- Tuck in your thumb
- Fold the fingers down repeatedly to symbolize trapping the thumb

ANDY SAYS

Choose a family code word that is as weird as possible, but don't pick something that's so bizarre it's hard to use naturally in a sentence.

HOME ALONE

IF YOU ARE HOME ALONE, YOU NEED TO KNOW WHAT TO DO IN AN EMERGENCY. THAT WAY, YOU WON'T PANIC WHEN SOMETHING GOES WRONG.

KNOW THE BASICS

There is no legal age in most countries when children are ready to stay home alone.

To be home alone, you must be able to use a phone so you can call for help, to work locks, and (if you're allowed) to use kitchen appliances.

BE PREPARED AND STAY IN TOUCH

IF A PARENT OR GUARDIAN IS LEAVING YOU ALONE, EVEN FOR ONLY A FEW MINUTES, THEY MUST:

BE ABLE TO STAY IN TOUCH

The adult must have a mobile phone so they can call you and receive calls from you.

PRACTICE WHAT TO DO IN AN EMERGENCY

Parents should practice with you what you should and shouldn't do in certain situations.

LEAVE IMPORTANT NUMBERS CLOSE BY

Your parents should always give you a couple of backup numbers to call in case they don't hear your phone ring, or if their phone is out of battery or has no signal. These could be a parent's mobile number, work number (if they've gone to work), and the number for a neighbor or nearby relative who can help you quickly if you need it.

HOME ALONE ESSENTIALS

WHAT IF THERE'S A FIRE OR ANOTHER EMERGENCY? If there's a fire, don't try to fight it yourself. Get out of the house, call the emergency services, and alert your neighbors.

WHAT SHOULD I DO IF A POWER SOCKET OR ELECTRICAL WIRE STARTS SMOKING? NEVER try to deal with it on your own. Treat a smoking wire as if it were a full-on fire.

HELP! I SMELL GAS! If you're home alone and you can smell gas, leave the property immediately. Don't switch off any lights on the way out or you might cause a spark which could ignite the gas. Don't even let anyone use the doorbell. If you have a mobile phone, call the emergency services, then warn the neighbors on either side.

WHAT DO YOU DO IF YOU ARE HOME ALONE AND A STRANGER COMES TO THE DOOR? NEVER open the door to a stranger. Unless you know who it is, the easiest thing is just not to answer the doorbell.

WHAT IF THE STRANGER WILL NOT GO AWAY?
Go somewhere in the apartment or house where you're out of sight and call your parents. If they don't answer, call your backup numbers or the police. Phone, hide, wait for help.

 If someone is trying to break into the house when you're home alone, call your parents then the police.

SURVIVING A HOUSE FIRE

HOUSE FIRES CAN BE DEADLY, AND AS ALWAYS PREPARATION IS KEY. IF YOU DO FIND YOURSELF TRAPPED, YOU MUST FIND A WAY TO GET OUTSIDE.

FAMILY FIRE RESPONSE PLAN

To ensure you are prepared, check and plan. Are there fire extinguishers in your house or apartment? How often are your smoke alarms tested? Are there escape ladders for the upper levels? You need to plan your emergency actions in advance.

HAVE A PLAN If you wake up in the night and smell smoke, what is the plan? Do you assemble at the front door? The back door?

ESCAPE If you can't get down the stairs, which upstairs room is the easiest to get out of? Which has the largest windows? Which window is closest to the ground, and which has the softest ground to land on? Are there any balconies or garage roofs which might make it easier to reach the ground safely? Which windows cannot be opened? It is way more difficult to climb out through a window you've had to break, and it is much more difficult to break a double-glazed window than a single-glazed one.

EMERGENCY EXIT It's probably going to be the front or back door, but what if you can't reach them because of fire or thick smoke? What then? Will the family leave by a window or gather in the bathroom?

MAKING YOUR ESCAPE

DEADLY SMOKE

Smoke is the biggest killer in house fires. Defend yourself with a wet towel or cloth over your nose and mouth.

STAY LOW, BE CAREFUL

Smoke fills a room from the ceiling down. As you pass from one room to another, close doors behind you to cut off the flow of air between rooms. Be careful when you open doors ahead of you. Look for any smoke coming through the cracks.

HELP, I'M ON FIRE!

If your clothes catch fire, cross your arms over your chest, drop to the floor, and smother the flames by rolling slowly over and over.

IF YOU'RE TRAPPED

If you're trapped in a room and it's impossible to escape, block as much smoke as you can using wet towels or clothes.

DON'T JUMP AND STAY OUT

Do not jump out of an upstairs window unless there's absolutely no other way. Use anything you can to get closer to the ground. Once everyone is accounted for, NEVER go back inside .

TRUE STORY

Arizona girl Samantha Christian, 10, saved her mother and brother on the day their home caught fire. She woke up to the sound of a huge fire in her room. She ran and got her mother before going right back inside to save her younger brother, who was four. She realized he couldn't get up, so she carried him out of the house. Afterward, Samantha said, "Clothes, metal, jewelry—all sorts of stuff can be replaced, but humans can't."

SAFE IN THE CITY

WHEN YOU ARE OUT AND ABOUT, BE SURE TO STICK TO YOUR PLANS.
DON'T GIVE IN TO PRESSURE TO DO SOMETHING YOU KNOW TO BE WRONG.

PEER PRESSURE

WHAT SHOULD YOU DO IF SOMEONE (EVEN A FRIEND) TRIES TO MAKE YOU DO THINGS YOU KNOW YOU AREN'T SUPPOSED TO DO? Say No! It doesn't matter whether it's an adult or another kid who's asking you. Tell your parents, a teacher, or a trusted adult.

WHAT SHOULD YOU DO IF A FRIEND DOES SOMETHING THEN TELLS YOU TO KEEP IT SECRET? You have to speak up. It's very important you tell your parents the truth about such things. This isn't just for your own good, but also to help others. How would you feel if bad things happened to others because you hadn't reported bad behavior?

SET THE EXAMPLE

WHAT SHOULD YOU DO IF YOUR FRIENDS ARE DOING SOMETHING YOU KNOW IS BAD? You know the difference between right and wrong, so always do the right thing, even if you're the only one doing it! And remember, the fact that ten people are doing the wrong thing doesn't make it right!

WHAT SHOULD YOU DO IF YOUR FRIENDS MAKE FUN OF YOU BECAUSE YOU WON'T DO IT? The right thing is always the right thing! Stick to your guns. If your friends really pressure you to join in, you have to ask yourself whether they're really friends. If the situation gets bad, you should call your parents and ask them to come and get you.

WHAT IF YOU ARE OUT AND ABOUT, SAY AT THE PARK, AND YOUR FRIEND WANTS TO GO SOMEWHERE YOU KNOW YOU DON'T HAVE PERMISSION TO GO? Stick to the plan! Kids sometimes think it's going to be okay if they leave an area they've been given permission to go to as long as they come back soon or don't go far. But imagine how horrible it would be for your parents if they needed to find you and you'd disappeared?

Like any other family plan, it's important to stick to arrangements. Stay where you said you were going to be, and stay there for as long as you said you were going to stay.

WHAT IF YOU DECIDE TO WALK HOME FROM A FRIEND'S HOUSE OR SCHOOL BY A DIFFERENT ROUTE FROM THE ONE YOU'VE AGREED WITH YOUR PARENTS?

1. Keep to any route that you have agreed with your parents. That way, they'll know where to look if anything happens to you. You might feel adventurous and decide to try a new route, but this could lead to disaster.

2. The most direct route is usually the best. Know what to do if anything unusual or weird did happen.

When you're walking home, it's best to stick to routes you know well.

WHAT IF YOU GET LOST WHEN YOU'RE OUT WITH YOUR PARENTS?

1. Approach a mother with children or anyone in uniform and ask them if they can take you to the information desk or to a security guard. If they don't have the time to do that, ask if they can phone your parents.

2. If no one is around who can help, go into a store where you can wait for them. Approach a security guard or someone working at checkout and ask if they can help.

MISSING THE BUS

If you were being met off the bus but fell asleep or missed your stop, follow these important steps.

DON'T PANIC and just jump off at the next stop. You might not know the area and could find yourself in a bad situation.

CALL WHOEVER was going to meet you if you have a phone and make a new plan.

NO PHONE, NO PROBLEM, tell the bus driver what's happened, and ask if they can call whoever was meeting you. They can come and get you.

REFUSE OFFERS OF LIFTS

School parents often try to be helpful and might think they're being kind if they offer you a lift home.

But you and your parents will probably already have a plan in place, so you must say No (very nicely!), and explain that you must wait for your arranged lift home.

If you're at a bus stop and they stop and offer you a lift, explain that your parents expect you to stick to the usual plan, but if you can contact your parents for permission, then it's fine.

Your parents might be happy for you to accept lifts from parents you know, but you should ask each time if they've checked with your parents.

ELEVATORS

WHEN AN ELEVATOR BREAKS DOWN, THE BIGGEST DANGER IS FROM PANIC. MAKE SURE YOU ARE THE ONE WHO MANAGES TO STAY CALM.

DON'T WORRY!

It is easy to panic inside a small elevator, but stay calm and make sure everyone else stays calm. Things are not as bad as they might appear.

TRY TO REASSURE anyone who shows signs of panic. Tell them it's impossible for a modern elevator to fall out of control down the shaft.

MODERN ELEVATORS are designed with plenty of ventilation, and there's no risk of running out of oxygen.

ANDY SAYS

Follow any emergency procedures that are usually found near the elevator buttons. Press the help button or use the telephone by the floor buttons and someone should answer. Follow their instructions.

AUTOMATIC BRAKES, usually fitted under the floor of the elevator, prevent falls from happening by clamping onto the steel guide rails that run down each side of the elevator shaft. The brakes will work even if there is a power cut and the lights go out. The best thing to do is to sit down and wait for help to arrive.

WHAT IF NO ONE ANSWERS THE HELP BUTTON? HERE ARE TEN THINGS TO REMEMBER.

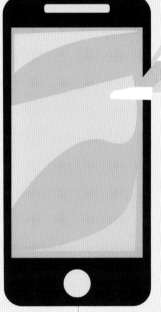

1. If you have a mobile phone, call any emergency number that's signposted, and if necessary, the emergency services.

2. If you have a mobile phone, call your parents to say what's happening.

3. Now try pressing each of the floor buttons one by one. Then try the "door open" button. You never know!

4. If you can see light through any gap between the elevator doors, the elevator has probably stopped near a floor. Watch for people moving and shout for help. Whatever you do, don't try to force the doors open yourself. If the elevator starts working when you are halfway out, things could turn nasty.

5. If you're alone, now is the time to sit down, and wait. There's not a lot more you can do anyway. Modern elevators don't have hatches in the ceiling you can escape through.

6. Go through your wallet, bag, or any reading matter you may have with you—anything to keep your mind off the situation.

7. If there are still people in the building, you'll want to get their help before they leave for the night. Shout and bang the inside walls of the elevator with a shoe or other solid object.

8. If there is no elevator engineer immediately available, rescues are usually handled by the fire service. Firemen will winch the elevator up or down to the nearest floor.

9. If it's an old elevator, there might be a hatch in the ceiling. Do not even think about climbing out. If the open hatch falls shut by accident, the elevator could move without warning.

10. In the incredibly unlikely event that nobody is responding to the alarm, and everyone has left the building, the worst-case scenario is that you could be in the elevator overnight. Try to enjoy it!

NEVER TRY TO ESCAPE FROM THE ELEVATOR WITHOUT HELP FROM AN EXPERT OUTSIDE!

HELP

91

TRAPPED IN A CAR

IF YOU ARE TRAPPED IN A CAR, QUICK THINKING MAY
BE NEEDED. STAY CALM AND THINK CLEARLY.

CAR IN THE WATER

Most cars will float for a while,
giving you time to save the day.
Immediately remove your seatbelt
so you are ready for action.

WHILE YOU ARE AFLOAT

As soon as your car enters the water,
release the door locks and switch on
all the lights as a signal.

1. If you can, open the doors before the car begins to sink and escape. You won't be able to open the doors once the car is partially submerged.

2. If the doors won't open, wind down your windows as quickly as possible. Climb out and swim to safety.

3. If you are unable to open your doors or windows, try to smash a window. Use something heavy like a wrench or the metal end of a headrest. Smash it at the corner as this is where the window is weakest. You can also buy special window breaking hammers that can be stored in a side pocket, glove compartment, or be Velcroed to the sun visor.

ONCE THE CAR SINKS

You are going to have to wait until
the car has filled with water before
you can open the doors.

1. Climb into the back seat because the front of the car, where the heavy engine is, will sink first.

2. Wait until the water has reached neck height. Then instruct everyone to take a big gulp of air.

3. Grasp the door handle ready for your getaway. Once the doors are completely submerged, they should open with a push. Open the door and escape.

4. If there are more than one of you in the car, form a human chain to make sure no one is left behind.

5. Swim up, breathing out as you go.

SNOWBOUND IN A CAR

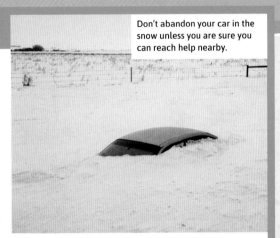

Don't abandon your car in the snow unless you are sure you can reach help nearby.

If you find yourself trapped in freezing conditions in a broken-down vehicle, the first rule is to keep calm. Consider each action carefully.

Stay awake and stay with your vehicle. Call emergency services if you have signal on your mobile phone.

Quickly get everything out of the trunk that will help to keep you warm and fed or help to dig through the snow.

Tie a marker to the top of your antenna, if you have one.

Only run the car engine if the exhaust can be kept clear of snow.

Regularly open windows on the side that is out of the wind to keep air fresh.

If you don't have blankets or a sleeping bag (tut tut!) use anything to keep your body warm.

Where many vehicles are stuck together, groups of motorists should gather together in the one best able to keep warm, or the one that is in the most prominent position for rescuers to see.

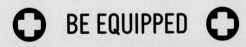

BE EQUIPPED

If you have to drive in freezing conditions, make sure you carry waterproof boots, warm coats, hats, and gloves inside the vehicle, as well as blankets, sleeping bags, thermos flasks of hot drinks, chocolate, and other food to keep energy up. Carry a shovel in the trunk of your car.

BULLIES

BULLIES ARE LIKE LUMPS OF DOG POOP—THEY ARE FOUND ANYWHERE YOU GO, AND THEY STINK. IT'S TIME TO STAND UP TO THEM!

STOP IT!

Bullies often have a lot of personal issues and they like to tease and scare other kids to make themselves feel big or more secure. But if a bully picks on you, remember: their issues are not your fault and they are not your problem.

BEING BULLIED is a really miserable experience, so don't just grin and bear it. It's tempting just to shrug it off and walk away, thinking it's harmless. It isn't.

WRITE DOWN exactly what the bully says or does and make a note of any witnesses to the bullying. That way you can give an adult an accurate account of what happened.

ANDY SAYS

If a bully picks on you, don't suffer in silence. Together, let's send a message that bullying is unacceptable.

HOW COME I'M THE ONE BEING PICKED ON?

Bullying is not your fault, and things will get better. Remember, bullies often act out of jealousy or because they think you're an easy target.

1. BE CONFIDENT

A lot of times bullies pick on people that they think won't stand up for themselves. Hold your head high!

2. JOIN A CLUB

Join the drama club, sports club, chess club, anything that plays to your strengths. When you surround yourself with people that share similar interests, all those other people become your army. Travel in packs, so you're never caught alone with a bully.

WHEN YOU SEE bullying or are being bullied, let the people doing it know that it's not okay. Just remember not to use harmful words or get physical. Stay calm and be respectful.

GET A TEACHER INVOLVED. Schools should be bully-free zones. No matter how alone you might feel, there is always someone you can talk to and someone who can help.

SPEAK OUT. If you need extra help, let a parent, guardian, or trusted adult know what's going on. The bullying will come to an end a lot more quickly if you tell someone what's going on.

MARTIAL ARTS OR SELF-DEFENSE CLASSES will help you feel more confident. However, you should never use violence against bullies. It will only make things worse. Leave their punishment to those in authority.

✱✱✱✱!

##!

✱✱✱✱✱!

###!

WHAT IF OTHERS ARE BEING BULLIED?

If you see someone else being bullied, you need to get an adult involved. Don't encourage bullying by laughing or walking away, relieved that you're not the victim. It only encourages the bully and makes the person being picked on feel worse. Instead, ask the person being picked on if they're okay.

Don't be afraid to let others know that you are a leader in stopping bullying. Be kind and treat others how you want to be treated and come to the aid of those in need.

ARE YOU OK?

BULLYING AT SCHOOL

Don't put up with it. Nobody has the right to make you feel unsafe, uncomfortable, or unhappy.

▼

Talk to your parents or guardians and your teacher. Your teacher may have no idea that you are being bullied, and the school will have an anti-bullying policy to tackle it. Keep reporting the bullying until it stops. If the bullying continues, tell them again.

If you feel you can't speak to your teacher, maybe a friend can do it for you. You can also speak to a school counselor, welfare officer, or nurse.

▼

If you're uncomfortable approaching someone at your school, there are other places to turn to. Helplines have people available to talk.

BULLYING OUSIDE SCHOOL

Talk to your parents or guardians, close relatives such as grandparents, aunties and uncles, or even your friends' parents. Youth workers and leaders may be able to help too.

▼

Tell a trusted adult—your parents or guardians, or a teacher. See also Cyberbullying (page 118).

SPEAKING OUT

Telling people that you're being bullied can be a tough thing to do. It can feel like admitting that you can't take care of yourself, but it isn't.

TELL YOUR PARENTS! Speaking with your parents can be tough, but look at it this way, you're being extremely brave and it can be one of the best things you can do. Only if you tell them can they help you bring the bullying to an end.

TELL A FRIEND! It can also be really helpful to tell a friend that you trust about the bullying. That way if the people who are bullying you approach you, your friend can act as a witness. They can also go with you for support when you talk to a teacher.

CHOKING

IF YOU SEE SOMEONE CHOKING, YOU MUST INTERVENE AS QUICKLY AS YOU CAN. YOU NEED TO CLEAR THEIR AIRWAY SO THAT THEY CAN BREATHE.

"5 AND 5" APPROACH

IF THE PERSON IS CHOKING AND CAN'T TALK, FOLLOW THESE STEPS
- 5 BLOWS TO THE BACK • THEN 5 ABDOMINAL THRUSTS (ALSO CALLED THE HEIMLICH MANEUVER)

BLOWS TO THE BACK:

1. Stand to the side and just behind a choking adult. For a child, kneel down behind.

2. Place one arm across the person's chest for support.

3. Bend the person over at the waist so that the upper body is parallel with the ground.

4. Deliver five separate back blows between the person's shoulder blades with the heel of your hand.

ABDOMINAL THRUSTS:

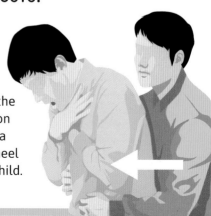

1. Stand behind the person. Place one foot slightly in front of the other for balance. Wrap your arms around the waist. Tip the person forward slightly. If a child is choking, kneel down behind the child.

ANDY SAYS

To prepare yourself for these situations, learn the Heimlich maneuver and CPR in a certified first-aid training course.

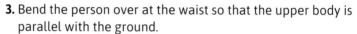

- **Lower the person** on his or her back onto the floor, arms to the side.
- **Clear the airway**. If a blockage is visible at the back of the throat or high in the throat, reach a finger into the mouth and sweep out the cause of the blockage. Don't try a finger sweep if you can't see the object.
- **Sit on their hips and face them.** Put one of your hands on top of the other and place the base of your palm between their belly button and lower ribs. Push upwards hard and repeat this several times until the airway is clear.
- **Be careful** not to push the food or object deeper into the airway, which can easily happen in young children.

BEGIN CPR
IF THE OBJECT REMAINS LODGED AND THE PERSON DOESN'T RESPOND, YOU MUST ENGAGE IN CPR (SEE PAGE 69). REMEMBER TO RECHECK THE MOUTH PERIODICALLY.

2. Make a fist with one hand. Position it slightly above the person's navel. Grasp the fist with the other hand. Press hard into the abdomen with a quick, upward thrust —as if you're trying to lift the person up.

TRUE STORY

Six-year-old Elspeth Mar was eating lunch at school in Sacramento, California, when her friend Aniyah starting choking. A piece of apple had wedged in Aniyah's airway. Elspeth stood up, grabbed Aniyah from behind, and performed the Heimlich maneuver on her. It only took one thrust for Aniyah to spit out the apple that had been blocking her windpipe. Elspeth explained that she'd learned the maneuver from a TV show.

3. Alternate between 5 blows and 5 thrusts until the blockage is dislodged. If you're the only rescuer, perform back blows and abdominal thrusts before calling the emergency services for help. If another person is available, have that person call for help while you perform first aid.

CROWD CRUSH

LARGE CROWDS AT PUBLIC EVENTS CAN SOMETIMES GET OUT OF CONTROL. THINK AHEAD AND AVOID THE CRUSH.

HOW TO AVOID A CROWD CRUSH

- At an event, explore the space around you long before there's any problem.

- Take a few seconds to note where the emergency exits are, and pick a couple of alternatives of your own, such as windows.

- A large crowd often acts like a herd. Most people will rush for the same doorway or gate that they used to enter the venue, so you need to look at alternative ways to get out.

- If possible, stay near the edge of the crowd, or position yourself near less obvious escape routes, such as a gap in a barricade. In an emergency, this will allow you to make a quick escape.

- At a sporting event, the safest place might be on the field, not trying to fight your way out through narrow turnstiles.

TIP Leave while you can. The longer you wait, the harder it will be to escape. When you start to feel uncomfortable in a crowd, that is the time to start thinking about leaving. Get out of the crowd while you still have enough room to move.

IF YOU ARE STUCK IN THE CROWD

1. GO WITH THE FLOW
When pushed, our natural instinct is to push back. Instead, let yourself be carried by the flow while always retaining your balance.

▼

2. MOVE AWAY FROM BARRIERS
The only time when going with the flow does not apply is if you're next to a wall, fence, or other solid object you can't climb up. If possible, move away from any walls, pillars, and fences.

▼

3. FIND A HIGH POINT
Don't forget to look up. You might find a quick escape by climbing a fence or getting up onto a ledge.

▼

4. MAKE LIKE A BOXER!
You have to create a little space around yourself, and the best way to do it is to bring your arms up in front of your chest like a boxer. Also keep your legs separated, one behind the other, for balance.

▼

5. AVOID NARROW HALLWAYS
Use one of the alternative escape routes you scoped out when you arrived.

6. COMMUNICATE CALMLY
If you're in a crowd of scared people, don't scream or do anything else that might scare them even more. Say calmly, "Please move back, give us space."

▼

7. TRY THE "ACCORDION" MOVE
After you're pushed forwards by the crowd, there's always a lull. This lull is your opportunity to use what experts call the "accordion" move to step diagonally between pockets of people.

▼

8. DON'T FALL DOWN!
Your top priority should be to stay on your feet. And don't stop for anything.

▼

IF YOU DO FALL, try to get up quickly. If it's impossible, try to crawl in the same direction as the crowd. If you can't do that either, you must protect yourself. Curl up into a ball on your side, keep your arms up to protect your lungs, and cover your head with your hands if you can.

"

ANDY SAYS

Stay human! Crowds tend to be heroic and compassionate. Make sure you don't knock somebody down and help others as much as you can.

"

DOG ATTACKS

AN AGGRESSIVE DOG CAN BE VERY SCARY. LOOK OUT FOR THE WARNING SIGNS AND FOLLOW THESE STEPS TO MAKE YOUR ESCAPE.

WHEN DO DOGS ATTACK?

IT'S VERY UNUSUAL for a stray dog to attack people. Most dog bites happen because pet dogs aren't trained or leashed properly. Their main targets are joggers, cyclists, or people who are trying to protect their own dogs.

ALWAYS STAY AWAY from strange dogs, and ask the owner's permission before patting their pet.

IF YOU ARE CONFRONTED by a dog that wants trouble, stay calm and do your best to defuse the situation.

WARNING SIGNS

If the dog approaches you with its body relaxed and a sloping curve in its midsection, it is probably not going to attack. A loping gait means the dog is playful and checking you out.

▼

Signs of aggression include a dog whose body is straight and stiff (head, shoulders, and hips in a line), and an even, steady run.

▼

Also watch out for: fur raised, growling, snarling, narrowed eyes, pulled-back ears lying flat against the head, or ears that are up and directed toward you.

IF CONFRONTED BY A DOG

STAND STILL and say "No!" in a firm tone.

DO NOT SCREAM, shout, or be aggressive. If the dog sees that it can't scare you, it might think you're not a person to mess with.

DON'T RUN. There's no way you'll outrun a dog.

AVOID SMILING. An aggressive dog sees you baring your teeth for a fight.

IF YOU ARE CYCLING, dismount and keep the bicycle between you and the dog. This will create a barrier. If a dog is attacking you, use the bicycle as a weapon to strike the dog.

NEVER TURN YOUR BACK TO THE DOG, but do not look directly at it. Eye contact communicates a challenge. Turn sideways to the dog, so you look less threatening, and you're not staring it down.

MAKING AN ESCAPE

- **If the dog turns** its head away when you do and its body looks more relaxed, keep backing away slowly. After a minute or two, if the dog doesn't follow you, walk away at a normal pace.
- **If there's a stick** or rock handy, try throwing it as far as you can. If you have nothing to throw, you can pretend you're picking something up from the ground and throw it far away. It might give you the necessary time to climb onto something.
- **Dogs can't climb!** Climb up a tree, a high fence, or even on top of a car or a mailbox.
- **Now you can risk** raising your voice—yell for help!

IF THE DOG ATTACKS

If worst comes to worst, be prepared to protect your face, throat, and chest. Curl your fingers into fists to prevent them from getting bitten. If the dog knocks you down, roll onto your stomach, tuck your knees in, and bring your hands up to your ears. Resist the urge to scream or roll away.

When you're safe, wash any wounds with soap and water and go straight to a hospital to get yourself checked out.

BEING FOLLOWED

BEING FOLLOWED CAN BE A VERY SCARY SITUATION. YOU NEED TO FIND HELP IMMEDIATELY. AND NEVER, EVER ACCEPT GIFTS FROM STRANGERS.

WHAT TO DO IF YOU THINK YOU'RE BEING FOLLOWED

1. KEEP CALM AND GET HELP

Go into a store or safe building. Try to see if they move away. If they don't, explain the situation to a security guard or other trusted adult, or call a family member if you have a phone. If you don't have a phone, ask a trusted adult if you can use theirs.

2. CALL THE POLICE

If you're not in a public place, head for one immediately. Crowds will stop someone from following you or approaching you. While you're on your way, call the police if you have a phone—or stop and ask someone if you can use theirs. If you see someone in uniform or a mother with children, ask if you can stay with them until the police arrive.

3. CONTACT PARENTS, FAMILY, OR FRIENDS

If you can't call the police, call or text parents, family, or friends who may be nearby. Plan to meet with a group of them as soon as you can, in a busy public area.

4. YELL!

If you feel immediately threatened, don't be embarrassed to yell! By simply yelling "Help me!" you could both scare off the offender and get someone to come to your assistance.

WHO CAN YOU TRUST?

Most strangers are nice, normal people. If you need help—whether you're lost, being threatened by a bully, or being followed by a stranger—the safest thing for you to do in many cases is to ask a stranger for help. So which strangers is it okay to trust?

SAFER STRANGERS: Usually, they will be wearing a uniform. They could be police officers, firemen, ambulance personnel, crossing guards, check-out assistants, bus drivers, or supermarket security staff.

SAFER BUILDINGS: Whenever possible, go to a public place to ask for help. If you're in difficulties and can't see a safe stranger outdoors, you should look for a safe building to go into. These could be banks, post offices, libraries, medical centers, shops, supermarkets, or leisure centers.

STRANGER DANGER

WHAT IF AN ADULT STRANGER IS ASKING FOR HELP?

If an adult asks you for help, say No, and leave.

NEVER GO WITH A STRANGER, ACCEPT ANY GIFTS, OR GET INTO A STRANGER'S CAR.

IF AN ADULT TRIES TO GRAB YOU

All good manners must go out of the window if you're in trouble. You are allowed to hit and scream —whatever it takes to get help.

Run away if you can, yell as loud as you can, and tell a trusted adult immediately what happened.

> ## ANDY SAYS
> If you're being followed by someone in a car, run in the opposite direction of the car.

BEING ROBBED

STREET ROBBERS ARE ON THE LOOKOUT FOR EASY TARGETS.
MAKE SURE THAT'S NOT YOU BY STAYING AWARE OF YOUR SURROUNDINGS.
AND IF YOU ARE ROBBED, DON'T TRY TO BE A HERO.

In public places, don't constantly stare at your phone.

AVOID THE DANGER

The best way to deal with a street robbery is to avoid it in the first place.

1. STAY IN BUSY AREAS. You're much less likely to be approached by someone on a main road than down a side street.

2. AVOID DARK ALLEYS AND SIDE STREETS. If you have to use unlit streets, always carry a bright flashlight. It allows you to identify potential threats, and the bright light can blind attackers long enough for you to run away.

3. STAY AWARE. Always know what's going on around you. Don't wander around wearing headphones or looking down at your phone.

4. IF YOU SEE A POTENTIAL THREAT, MOVE TO SAFETY. Cross the road or change route altogether if you don't like the look of what's up ahead. But don't divert down dark alleys or dimly lit streets: safety means well-lit and populated areas.

5. KEEP YOUR DISTANCE FROM POTENTIAL ATTACKERS.

IF YOU ARE ROBBED

GIVE THEM WHAT THEY WANT
• WHATEVER YOU DO, DON'T FIGHT BACK

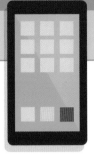

MOST BAD GUYS just want money from you. If you give them what they want, they'll leave you alone. When you do give them the items though, do so in a way that means you can keep your distance. Throw it to them if necessary.

YOUR PARENTS might consider giving you a dummy wallet with some folding money in it. The golden rule is, always have something you can hand over.

MAKE NOISE. People who do this kind of thing want to do their work as discreetly as possible. Use a loud voice if you have to interact with them and you might scare them off.

TRY TO REMEMBER DETAILS. It's going to be a scary experience, but do your best to remember details about your attacker's appearance so you can tell the police. What clothes are they wearing, what color is their hair, do they have tattoos?

 TIME TO RESIST

THE ONLY TIME TO FIGHT BACK IS IF THE ATTACKER IS DEMANDING THAT YOU GET INTO A CAR OR GO WITH THEM DOWN A SIDE STREET OR ALLEY. IF YOU'RE TOLD TO GET INTO A VEHICLE, THIS ISN'T A STREET ROBBERY. ONLY IN THIS SITUATION, FIGHT LIKE YOUR LIFE DEPENDS ON IT—BECAUSE IT MIGHT.

EMERGENCY BAG

A BUG-OUT BAG (ALSO CALLED A GRAB BAG) IS A DAYSACK OR BACKPACK FULL OF EMERGENCY ITEMS IN CASE YOU NEED TO FLEE YOUR HOME. HERE'S WHAT TO PUT IN IT.

PACKING THE BAG

A home-made kit has some real advantages over even the best-designed commercially available kits. Not only can you tailor it to your needs, but you will know each item and why you included it. What are the contents of a good grab bag?

- A copy of this book!
- First aid kit
- Medication
- Cash
- Car keys
- House door keys
- Spare clothes
- Flashlight and headlamp

- Toiletries
- Pen and notepad
- Batteries

- Small battery or hand-cranked radio, if no mobile phone
- Bottled water and emergency food (remember to replace it when the expiry dates are reached)
- Important documents (stored in a waterproof bag within another waterproof bag)
- At least 12 feet (4 m) of paracord
- With your

parents' permission, a knife is a good idea
- Also with your parents' permission, a lighter
- A compass
- A can of spray bandages (adhesive bandages can get wet and drop off)
- Duct tape (this has hundreds of uses)

- Scissors
- Safety pins

- Portable water filtration system
- Chemical water purification tablets or drops
- Collapsible water bag or bladder
- Stainless steel water bottle
- Stainless steel bowl/pot
- Utensils
- Collapsible fishing kit
- Portable stove
- Fuel for stove/fire (solid fuel, fire starters, ferro rod, waterproof matches)
- Multipurpose tool with knife, can opener, screwdriver, etc.
- Waterproof Ziploc bags
- Lightweight tent or bivvy bag
- Sleeping bag
- Ground pad
- Emergency waterproof blanket or space blanket
- Hand warmers
- Rain poncho or other durable waterproof outer shell layer
- Hat for warmth (winter) or sun protection (summer)
- Spare set of glasses, if you wear them
- Antibacterial wipes and ointment
- Sunscreen
- Soap
- Toothbrush and toothpaste
- Travel towel
- Toilet paper/wet wipes

A survival blanket—a compact and lightweight sheet of aluminized non-stretch polyester, which will provide instant protection from the elements.

High-carbohydrate foods, canned foods, candy, crackers, unsalted nuts, dried fruit, muesli bars, glucose tablets, or cookies.

Rubber tubing – this is very useful for obtaining drinking water from difficult or inaccessible places. You can also use it in a solar still. An appropriate size would be 3 feet (1 m) of 5 mm tubing.

QUIZ

1 WHAT IS THE MOST IMPORTANT SURVIVAL SKILL?

A. Sleeping

B. Deep breathing

C. Calling the emergency services

2 WHAT IS THE MOST DANGEROUS PART OF A HOUSE FIRE?

A. Smoke

B. Ash

C. Flames

3 WHICH OF THESE IS AN EMERGENCY SIGNAL?

A. Fingers folded over your thumb

B. Thumbs up

C. Middle two fingers and thumb on the palm

4 WHAT CAN A MODERN ELEVATOR NOT DO?

A. Open

B. Fall

C. Allow cell phone signals

5 WHAT'S ANOTHER NAME FOR THE ABDOMINAL THRUSTS THAT CAN SAVE SOMEONE FROM CHOKING?

A. Kobayashi Maru

B. The Heimlich Maneuver

C. The Voight-Kampff Test

6 IF YOU'RE SNOWBOUND IN A CAR, WHERE SHOULD YOU PUT A MARKER?

A. Headlights

B. Wing mirror

C. Antenna

7 SAFELY STEPPING DIAGONALLY THROUGH LARGE CROWDS IS ALSO KNOWN AS:

A. Crowdsourcing

B. The "Accordion" Move

C. Market Deeping

8 WHICH OF THESE SIGNS MEANS A DOG MAY BE AGGRESSIVE?

A. Relaxed body

B. Pulled-back, flat ears

C. Wagging tail

9 WHICH OF THESE CAN HELP YOU GET DRINKING WATER FROM INACCESSIBLE PLACES?

A. Rubber tubing

B. Concave mirror

C. Duct tape

10 WHICH OF THESE IS NOT A HIGH-CARBOHYDRATE FOOD FOR AN EMERGENCY BAG?

A. Cookies

B. Chocolate

C. Bacon

Answers on page 143

SURVIVING ONLINE

THE INTERNET

THE INTERNET IS AMAZING, CONNECTING US TO PEOPLE AROUND THE WORLD. BUT IT CAN ALSO BE DANGEROUS, AND YOU NEED TO PROTECT YOURSELF.

HIDDEN DANGERS

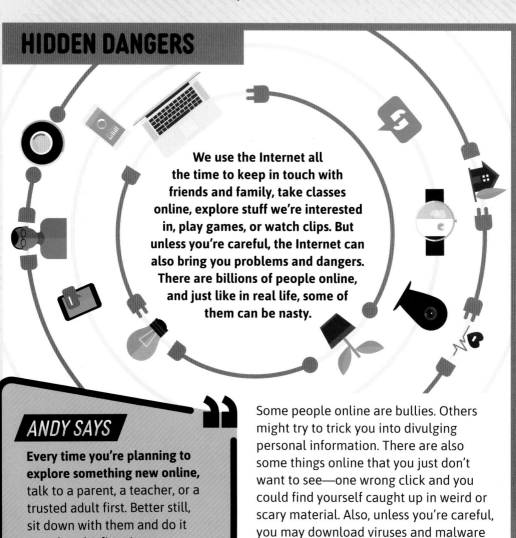

We use the Internet all the time to keep in touch with friends and family, take classes online, explore stuff we're interested in, play games, or watch clips. But unless you're careful, the Internet can also bring you problems and dangers. There are billions of people online, and just like in real life, some of them can be nasty.

ANDY SAYS

Every time you're planning to explore something new online, talk to a parent, a teacher, or a trusted adult first. Better still, sit down with them and do it together the first time.

Some people online are bullies. Others might try to trick you into divulging personal information. There are also some things online that you just don't want to see—one wrong click and you could find yourself caught up in weird or scary material. Also, unless you're careful, you may download viruses and malware that can damage your computer.

INTERNET RULES

These are some simple ways to protect yourself and your computer and stay safe online.

DON'T: Post pictures, videos, or content about your friends, family, or school without their permission. Always, always, always ask them first.

DON'T: Talk to people online that you've never met before, unless you've checked first with a parent.

DON'T: Share your passwords or log-in information with anyone except your parents, not even your best friend.

DON'T: Accept anyone as a friend on social media who isn't a friend in real life. Above all, **TRUST YOUR OWN INSTINCTS.**

DO: Ask your parents before creating an account on a new social media platform.

DO: Use the privacy settings for ALL social media accounts to make sure your content, personal information, and location are private.

DO: Tell your parents or a teacher right away if you come across pictures, videos, comments, or anything else online that makes you feel uncomfortable or in danger.

CHATROOMS

SOME STREAMING SITES LET YOU CHAT LIVE.
BUT DO YOU REALLY KNOW WHO YOU'RE CHATTING WITH?

NEVER TRUST A PROFILE PIC!

Adults called "predators" pretend to be kids and they might have a child's picture on their profile.

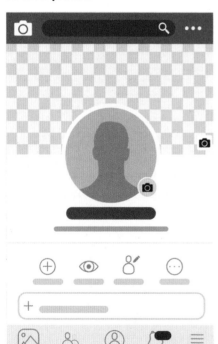

THINK FIRST before you "friend" any person you just met online, especially if that person is asking you questions about your life.

BE VERY CAREFUL about joining private chat rooms.

IF ANYONE in a chat room ever starts talking about something that makes you feel uncomfortable, save the conversation or screenshot it, then block them and sign off. Tell a parent, teacher, or trusted adult.

NEVER GIVE OUT personal information such as your home address, email address, or phone numbers.

TIP If you don't know someone in real life, don't add them as a friend online, no matter how nice they are to you.

GROOMER ALERT!

ONLINE GROOMERS ARE ADULTS WHO SPEND DAYS OR WEEKS GAINING THE TRUST OF A CHILD BEFORE ASKING THE CHILD TO DO THINGS THEY WOULDN'T NORMALLY WANT TO DO.

A groomer will pretend to be really interested in everything you say. They might ask about your favorite singers or bands, for example, and say that they really like them too.

▼

A groomer might start saying bad things about your teachers, or even your family and friends. They want you to stop trusting other people and trust them instead.

▼

A groomer might talk about things that make you feel uncomfortable. They might say they'll stop talking to you if you don't do what they ask.

A groomer might ask you to keep secrets and not to tell your parents, teachers, or friends what you chat about.

▼

A groomer might threaten to share things you've sent or said to them unless you share more.

▼

A groomer might ask you to chat in private. Most dangerous of all, they might ask you to meet them in real life.

  ## WHAT TO DO

IF YOU THINK SOMEONE'S TRYING TO GROOM YOU, FOLLOW THESE STEPS

- Trust your instincts. If something feels wrong, it nearly always is wrong.
- Just stop talking to them.
- Save or screenshot your conversations. The more information you can give the police, the easier it is for them to track down the groomer.

- Speak about it IMMEDIATELY to a parent, teacher, or adult you trust, and allow that adult to handle the situation. If you don't feel able to do that, call the police or a helpline. Don't feel embarrassed or ashamed about what's happened. If a groomer is trying to get at you, it is never ever your fault.

CYBERBULLYING

CYBERBULLIES USE COMPUTERS OR MOBILE PHONES TO BE MEAN TO OTHER PEOPLE. LIKE OTHER FORMS OF BULLYING, WE CAN PUT A STOP TO IT.

HOW TO SPOT CYBERBULLYING

In real life, you can walk away from a bully, but it can be hard to walk away online. If you encounter the examples below, you are being cyberbullied.

SPREADING LIES about you or someone else, or sending rude, mean, or threatening texts, emails, or online messages.

SHARING VIDEOS OR PHOTOS that make fun of you or posting comments and messages that look as if they come from someone else.

IF SOMEONE ELSE IS THE VICTIM OF CYBERBULLYING, SHOW THEM YOU CARE. LET THEM KNOW YOU'VE SEEN WHAT IS HAPPENING AND THAT, IF THEY WANT YOU TO, YOU WILL HELP THEM REPORT IT.

HOW TO STOP A CYBERBULLY

Save the page or take a screenshot where you see bullying happen. This can be used as evidence to show your parents or a teacher.

▼

Report bullying to a parent or a teacher, and they will help you report it to the social media platform where it happened. Tell them how you came in contact with that person, and what conversations or messages happened. Don't worry about reporting it. The authorities are there to help and have special methods to find the guilty person.

▼

Do not respond to a cyberbully in any way. Just like in real life, if you ignore a bully, they'll usually get bored and move on to someone else. But even if they move on, it's important to report them!

▼

If you can, block the person from your social media or gaming account, or block them as a caller if you have a mobile phone. Unfriend and unfollow them, and block them from seeing any more of what you do online. If your parents or teachers advise it, get them to help you change your email address or account profile.

▼

It's good to talk. You won't feel singled out by nasty messages if you talk to your friends about what's happened. You might find that the cyberbully is targeting them as well. If everyone reports cyberbullying, we can put an end to it.

DOXING

WHAT IS "DOXING", AND WHAT CAN YOU DO TO STOP IT FROM HAPPENING TO YOU?

WHAT IS DOXING?

Doxing (sometimes it's spelled "doxxing") occurs when someone finds out some of your personal information and publishes it online. It's a horrible thing to do, and it's pathetic, but a doxer's aim is usually just to embarrass you.

This is the worst part: if the doxer found that information somewhere else online, it's not against the law to publish it again, unless they're using the information to make you do something or to pay them to stop doing it!

PROTECT YOURSELF AGAINST DOXING

DO: Make sure ALL your social media accounts are set to private.

DO: Turn off ALL the location settings on your accounts and on ALL of your devices.

DON'T: Give out personal information about yourself online. This is what doxers are looking for:

- **Your real name**
- **Your cell phone number or home landline number**
- **Your home address**
- **Your parents' credit card numbers**
- **Your parents' bank account numbers**
- **Personal letters**
- **Personal photographs**
- **Social media profiles**

WHAT TO DO IF SOMEONE DOXES YOU

1. KEEP A RECORD

Save the page or make a screenshot of any threats.

2. CHANGE PASSWORDS

Change all of your passwords and security questions.

3. REPORT IT

Tell a parent or teacher and ask them to help you report the doxing attack to the platform where your personal information has been posted.

4. GO TO THE POLICE

If your home address is published online or a doxer makes personal threats against you, it's very serious. Your parents might want to talk to the police about what to do next.

IF A DOXER HAS PUBLISHED YOUR PARENTS' BANK ACCOUNT OR CREDIT CARD DETAILS, TELL YOUR PARENTS IMMEDIATELY. THEY WILL NEED TO REPORT THIS TO THEIR BANK AND CHANGE THE PASSWORDS FOR THEIR ONLINE ACCOUNTS.

SOCIAL MEDIA

MANY OF US STAY IN TOUCH VIA SOCIAL MEDIA. BUT BE SURE YOU HAVE PERMISSION BEFORE SIGNING UP, AND KEEP YOUR PRIVATE LIFE OFFLINE.

CAN I SIGN UP?

If you're under 13 and using Facebook or WhatsApp without asking permission, you really should get out of there!

When a social network sets an age limit, they do it for a reason. It means that some of the content may not be suitable for younger children. If you think it's funny or big to ignore their rules, be warned: if you break the platforms' rules, they aren't responsible for anything that happens to you while you're on their site. And if they find out you're too young, they can delete your account, remove all your posts and pictures, and stop you from rejoining in the future. Are you sure it's worth the risk?

Besides that, not telling your parents what social media you have joined is RISKY. Your parents might take away all your devices, or even just change the password to deny you access! Again, not worth the risk, is it?

Having said all that, adults need to be realistic. Many kids use social media, but if you want to join a platform that has age limits, the big rule is to talk it over with your parents. They always have your back, so let them decide.

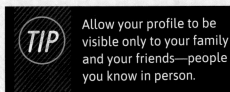
BE PRIVATE!

Make sure your location is not visible on any social media account! Turn OFF geo location on your devices. If you don't know how to do it, ask someone who does.

GOLDEN RULES

- **NEVER** give out your real name.
- **NEVER** say where you live.
- **NEVER** say where your school is.

Chat

Feed

Mail

SMS

Share

Search

Tag

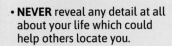

- **NEVER** reveal any detail at all about your life which could help others locate you.
- **NEVER** post photos, especially ones wearing your school's uniform, or any that could identify where you live. Photos taken on a digital camera or mobile phone have information embedded in them about where the picture was taken, and groomers can use this.

ONLINE GAMING

ONLINE GAMING IS SO MUCH FUN, IT CAN REALLY EAT UP YOUR FREE TIME. KEEP IT FUN BY STAYING SAFE, AND DON'T FORGET YOUR REAL-LIFE FRIENDS!

IN-GAME PURCHASES

You have to be an adult to own a credit card you have complete control over. However, some kids use their parents' credit cards to buy things online, download games, or make in-app purchases. Don't abuse their trust!

YOU'D NEVER STEAL from your parents' purse or wallet, would you? If you think about it, that's exactly what you're doing if you use their credit cards without their permission.

YOUR PARENTS have probably stored their card details on certain sites, such as Amazon, so they have easy, one-click options for shopping. That doesn't mean you can just do a few clicks of your own without asking them first. Remember, your parents have to pay for everything that gets charged to their credit cards, with real money.

WHEN YOU DOWNLOAD a video game, your personal information could be stolen, you could be a victim of cyberbullying, or your parents' bank details might be misused. If that happens, it'll be a very long time until they trust you again!

SAFE GAMING

WHEN GAMING ONLINE, FOLLOW THESE SIMPLE STEPS TO KEEP SAFE.

DO: Tell your parents if you want to buy a game online and let them decide if it's appropriate for you.

DO: Only make online purchases and join paid websites if you have your parents' permission.

DO: Only download legitimate apps from either the App Store or Play Store.

DO: Use a false name while playing a game—a name that does not say who you are, how old you are, or anything that might reveal your identity.

DO: Talk to your parents immediately if anything unusual happens while you're gaming, or anything makes you feel uncomfortable.

DO: Immediately tell your parents and block anyone who sends you inappropriate messages.

DO: Fix a time limit for yourself for playing a game on PC or consoles. Meet your friends in real life instead!

DON'T: Accept a "friend" request from a stranger in an online game.

DON'T: Share your personal information—not even your age or date of birth.

DON'T: Enter your parents' credit card details into a game without telling them.

DON'T: Download any game or app yourself.

DON'T: Play any game where someone asks you to do weird things.

DON'T FORGET!

1. STAY ANONYMOUS

Never give away personal information. When you're totally wrapped up in a game, it's easy to forget and give your real name or phone number to another player. And just like in a chat room, don't say things you wouldn't say to people face-to-face.

2. BLOCK AND REPORT

Most games have blocking features that allow you to block players if they make you feel uncomfortable. Many games also have reporting features where you can report inappropriate behavior to the game administrators—use them!

3. KEEP TALKING

If other players are inappropriate, talk to your parents or a trusted adult. (If your parents threaten to take the game away because of the behavior of others, remind them nicely that you have been honest and shouldn't be punished for it.)

ARE YOU GAMING TOO MUCH?

IF YOU THINK OR DREAM about a game when you're not playing it, this is a sign that it's time to cut down your game hours and either phone a real friend for a chat or go and play a real game outside.

IRRITABLE OR MOODY when you can't play? Do you control your gaming or does it control you? Do you play because you cannot stop?

ARE YOU LOSING INTEREST in other activities, such as playing sports or taking the dog for a walk?

JUST ONE MORE GAME . . .?
Are you being sneaky or dishonest, such as lying about the amount of time you spend online? Are you risking schoolwork or real-life relationships to give yourself more gaming time?

KNOW WHEN TO STOP

Game for less than two hours a day and preferably not at all on school days. Keep gaming as a weekend treat—and even then, take regular breaks.

▼

Do your homework and get your exercise first. Move your gaming device from your bedroom to a "public" room where there are others. No tech during meals or car rides—it's rude!

▼

Hand over your devices one hour or more before bedtime. Late-night screen time can mess with your sleep patterns and leave you feeling grouchy the next day.

▼

Have a discussion with your parents about how and when you will stop. They might not know that once you have started a match, you will lose standing and let your teammates down if you suddenly quit!

THE ULTIMATE PASSWORD

PASSWORDS ARE ONE OF THE MOST IMPORTANT ASPECTS OF INTERNET SAFETY, AND THAT'S WHY THIS SECTION IS SO LONG!

LOCK YOUR DEVICES

Your house or apartment has a front door, right? The door has a lock, maybe two or three. Without keys to those locks, outsiders can't enter. So imagine how you'd feel if there were no locks on your front door, and strangers could just come and go as they pleased. Not great, is it?

Your password is your lock to keep strangers out of your computer and other devices, and out of private spaces such as your email and social media sites.

When you join a new website or platform, you're usually asked to create a username and password. It's very important to create a strong password that's not easy for others to figure out, and it's just as important that you never, ever share it with anyone except a parent.

WHAT SHOULD I DO IF SOMEONE HACKS MY ACCOUNT OR MY EMAIL?

YOU NEED TO ACT AS SOON AS YOU FIND OUT YOUR ACCOUNT IS HACKED.

Password

Weak

Password

Strong

Long passwords are stronger than short ones, and adding special characters can also help.

1. TELL YOUR PARENTS or a teacher immediately.

▼

2. CHANGE THE PASSWORD immediately, if you can access the password page on your account.

▼

3. CHANGE OTHER PASSWORDS if you use the same password on other online accounts (bad idea!). You must access them all immediately and change them.

▼

4. DON'T TELL any of these new passwords to anyone except your parents.

▼

5. CHECK YOUR SETTINGS and make sure all your accounts are set to private.

6. CONTACT THE APP DEVELOPERS if it's an app that has been hacked. Ask an adult to contact the app developers to let them know.

▼

7. CONTACT AFFECTED PEOPLE if it looks as though the hacker has sent people messages from your account. Contact those people and tell them what's happened, and apologize. They'll be fine about it—it's happened to all of us at some time or another!

▼

8. REPORT IT if anyone ever demands you tell them your password. Tell your parents or a teacher.

PASSPHRASES

A PHRASE OF THREE RANDOM WORDS WILL PRODUCE A VERY STRONG, UNIQUE PASSWORD.

Don't use word combinations that others can easily guess, such as your name: e.g. Alice Jane Smith. Make sure it's a truly random combination of words. For instance:

> **scotlandterrificbiscuit**

Sometimes a site will insist that you include capital letters, numbers, symbols, and characters in your password. In this case, just add them in between your words. For instance:

> **Scotland's5terrific@biscuits**

Many websites insist on a minimum number of characters for passwords anyway, but the longer the password you choose, the harder it is for a hacker to crack—so now's the time to practice all those long words you had to learn for spelling tests! And again, a passphrase is better than a password.

 TIP
When choosing your passphrase, be very careful not to include personal information. Anything that someone knows or could guess about you is a terrible choice.

NEVER USE: your own name, your pet's name, your parents' names, your hometown, your place of birth, your favorite sport or favorite team's name.

> Scotland!
> Terrific
> biscuit!

DON'T let your browser store your passphrases. Most browsers will offer to store your passwords for you, autofilling forms when you need them. It's tempting to let them do that, but malware can get into your device and steal the passwords you have stored in your browser. Don't make life easy for hackers!

DON'T write down your passphrases. You might be tempted to write a list of your passphrases on a piece of paper somewhere. And to be fair, writing down a list of unique, strong passphrases is better than using the same easy-to-crack password on all your websites! But unless you have a terrible memory, it's not recommended.

CHANGING PASSWORDS

In the old days, you used to be told to change your passwords regularly, and in fact many organizations still enforce regular password changes.

However, the UK's National Cyber Security Centre (NCSC) now recommends that you DO NOT change passwords unless you have to. The reason is that it is now recognized that people don't like having to come up with new passwords, and just tend to recycle old ones. Terrible idea!

So: don't change passwords/passphrases for the sake of it. If you've got a strong passphrase you haven't used anywhere else, it will protect your account for a long time.

NEVER SHARE YOUR PASSPHRASES

If you allow someone to have your password, you are giving them permission to enter your account! You're giving them the key to your front door! Your best friend is probably a great person, but what if you fell out as friends, or they decided to prank you by going into your account and posting something silly?

The only person you should ever give your password to is a parent.

REMEMBER
- USE UNIQUE PASSWORDS ON EACH SITE
- A PASSPHRASE IS BEST
- DON'T USE PERSONAL INFORMATION
- DON'T CHANGE PASSWORDS REGULARLY

CELL PHONES

A CELL PHONE IS YOUR MOST PERSONAL PIECE OF TECH.
SO BE CAREFUL HOW YOU USE IT!

PHONE SAFETY

Most children aren't given a cell phone until they start middle school, though some might get one in the last year of elementary school if they make their own way to school. However, if you do have a phone, there are some important rules for your safety.

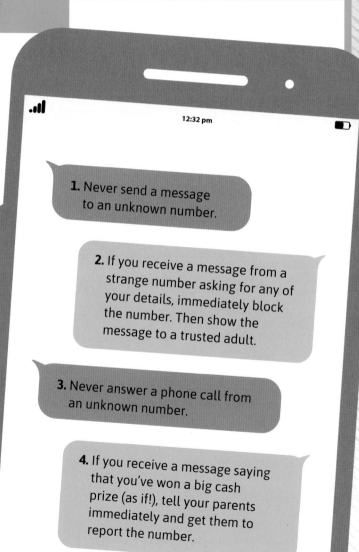

12:32 pm

1. Never send a message to an unknown number.

2. If you receive a message from a strange number asking for any of your details, immediately block the number. Then show the message to a trusted adult.

3. Never answer a phone call from an unknown number.

4. If you receive a message saying that you've won a big cash prize (as if!), tell your parents immediately and get them to report the number.

12:32 pm

5. Never click on a random link you receive in a message. It could take you to a site that plants malware.

6. Always use a screen lock so your phone's contents are protected if it's lost or stolen.

7. If your device is lost or stolen, immediately report it to the police.

8. Never share your password with anyone.

9. Protect your phone with FindMyPhone or a similar app. If it's lost or stolen, you might be able to trace it.

Q W E R T Y U I O P
S D F G H J K L

STAY OUT OF TROUBLE

WHEN TEXTING

Texting inappropriate messages or pictures can be against the law, and you could find yourself in serious trouble. They can also be transferred to others with the click of a button and end up on billions of devices. A hurtful text or private photo could cause someone a great deal of pain or trouble, even if you just forward it, and you don't want that, do you?

MALWARE

EVERY TIME YOU CONNECT TO THE INTERNET, YOUR DEVICE IS OPEN TO ALL KINDS OF CYBER NASTIES THAT CAN HARM IT OR WRECK IT COMPLETELY.

WHAT IS MALWARE?

Malware is any harmful software that finds its way into your computer without you knowing about it or agreeing to it. Malware includes viruses, "Trojan horses," "worms," "adware," and "spyware."

A lot of malware is just annoying—it's slipped onto your computer by companies that want to learn more about you so they can sell you stuff. But adware and spyware can clog up your computer and make it run slowly. R-e-a-l-l-y r-e-a-l-l-y slowly. Your parents won't be happy, guaranteed! An even bigger problem than a slow computer is the danger that, through malware, a hacker could get hold of private details about you or your parents, especially their credit card information.

SPREADING VIRUSES

VIRUSES ARE THE VERY WORST KINDS OF MALWARE. SOME VIRUSES CAN SPREAD FROM DEVICE TO DEVICE, MAKING THEM HARD TO USE OR BREAKING THEM ALTOGETHER.

PROTECT YOUR DEVICES

THESE ARE TEN GOLDEN RULES TO HELP KEEP YOUR DEVICES SAFE.

1. **Make sure you have a "firewall,"** which is something your parents will probably need to set up.

2. **Make sure you have good virus protection software** such as Norton, McAfee, or Intego's VirusBarrier, and make sure it updates.

3. **Get your parents to install a free adware checker on your computer,** such as Scanguard or Total AdBlock, and remind them to run adware/spyware scans every week or so.

4. **Use an email program that scans all emails for incoming threats.**

5. **NEVER click on links or download attachments in emails or texts from people you don't know.** If a link or attachment seems to come from a friend, check with them first to make sure they really did send it.

6. **Don't install any program directly from a website or email**. It's much safer to download from the Apple App Store or Google Play App Store.

7. **Don't install any free "toolbars" you are offered for your browser**.

8. **You shouldn't download files without permission anyway, but definitely stay away from file-sharing sites** that offer you pirated music or books.

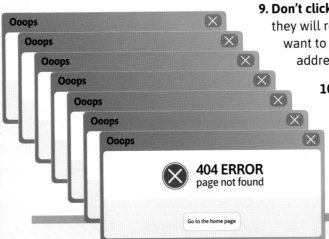

9. **Don't click on links within a website** as they will redirect you to places you don't want to go. It's safer to type a web address directly into your browser.

10. **Be very careful not to click buttons on pop-up screens** without showing a parent first—or any button anywhere that wants you to make a decision.

SEARCHING ONLINE

YOU CAN COME ACROSS ALL KINDS OF THINGS ON THE INTERNET,
SO MAKE SURE YOU'RE SEARCHING SAFELY.

THE GOOD AND THE BAD

The Internet is the most amazing source of free information in history. But...

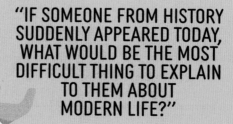

"IF SOMEONE FROM HISTORY SUDDENLY APPEARED TODAY, WHAT WOULD BE THE MOST DIFFICULT THING TO EXPLAIN TO THEM ABOUT MODERN LIFE?"

The answer is amazingly that you have a device in your pocket that is capable of accessing the entirety of information known to humanity. And you use it to look at pictures of kittens and get into arguments with people!

Unfortunately, there's good information and bad information, and that includes images and videos of inappropriate adult stuff that kids shouldn't be exposed to until they're over 18.

SAFER SEARCHING

Parents and teachers have a lot of worries about kids using Google and other online search engines. One of the biggest is the huge amount of scary, nasty, or illegal stuff that can pop up on kids' screens without them looking for it.

THERE'S A LOT THAT YOU and your parents can do to make a computer or other device much safer to use. Most browsers, such as Chrome, Firefox, and Safari, have Parental Controls. Parents can set filters to stop inappropriate sites from appearing in searches.

SEARCH

THE BEST WAY TO AVOID coming across unwanted stuff is to use a kid-friendly search engine. Google has Google Safe Search. Other kid-safe search engines include: KidsClick; Ask for Kids; Yahoo! Kids, and AOL Kids. Find the one that's best for you and save it on your desktop, then use it whenever you're online.

SPECIAL PARENTAL CONTROL SOFTWARE is also a way for parents to feel safer. This allows them to filter out inappropriate sites and to keep track of the sites every user of the computer is visiting.

THE EASIEST and best thing parents can do is to have a rule that kids can only use the Internet in a part of the house where there are other people. You'll soon find that doing your surfing with your parents in the same room helps everyone feel safer.

TEN GOLDEN RULES OF THE INTERNET

HERE IS A ROUNDUP OF THE THINGS WE'VE TALKED ABOUT TO MAKE SURE YOU STAY SAFE ONLINE.

1. HONESTY

Be honest with your parents and teachers about everything you do and search for online. Report anything that makes you feel uncomfortable.

2. PROTECT YOUR COMPUTER

Get your parents to protect your computer with good, up-to-date virus protection.

3. NEVER SHARE PASSWORDS

Passwords are absolutely private and should never be shared, except with your parents.

4. REPORT CYBERBULLIES

Cyberbullies are cowards. You can help put a stop to bullying by reporting people who are unkind to you or anyone else.

5. NEVER CLICK ON LINKS

Never click on links, attachments, or anything else in emails or on websites unless you're absolutely sure the material is safe AND have asked your parents' permission.

6. DOUBLE-CHECK

Be careful about believing anything you see, read, or hear online. Always try to double-check anything you learn on the Internet before you treat it as a fact.

7. KNOW YOUR REAL FRIENDS

"Friending" people online that you don't know in real life can put you at risk. It's best only to "friend" people who are your real friends.

8. PROTECT YOUR PROFILE

Make sure you have checked your privacy settings to ensure that only your true friends can see your online profile.

9. NOTHING ONLINE IS PRIVATE

Nothing you do online—even private messages—is actually private, so remember the Grandma Test.

10. DON'T SHARE PERSONAL STUFF

NEVER share personal information online or in an app. This means not revealing your full name, home address, name of your school, or photos of you wearing school uniform.

QUIZ

1 **WHAT SHOULD YOU DO BEFORE STARTING A NEW SOCIAL MEDIA ACCOUNT?**

A. Check with your parents

B. Check your Internet connection

C. Check your phone camera

2 **WHO SHOULD YOU REPORT CYBERBULLYING TO?**

A. Your Internet service provider

B. A YouTuber

C. A parent or teacher

3 **WHAT IS "DOXING"?**

A. Fingers folded over your thumb

B. Publishing someone's personal information online

C. Hacking a bank account

4 **WHAT SHOULD YOU NEVER REVEAL ONLINE?**

A. Your real name

B. Your favorite color

C. Your star sign

5 **WHAT COULD BE A SIGN THAT YOU'RE GAMING TOO MUCH?**

A. Sweating

B. Dry skin

C. Dreaming about games

6 A PASSWORD IS A BIT LIKE A…

A. Key to your house

B. Fast car

C. Open window

7 WHAT'S A GOOD WAY TO GENERATE A STRONG PASSWORD?

A. Your pet's name

B. Use three random words

C. Your mother's maiden name

8 WHAT IS MALWARE?

A. Broken equipment

B. Dangerous clothing

C. Harmful software

9 WHICH OF THESE WON'T MAKE AN INTERNET SEARCH SAFE?

A. Using parental controls

B. Wearing a blindfold

C. Using a child-friendly search engine

10 YOU SHOULD ONLY "FRIEND" PEOPLE WHO…

A. Are the same age as you

B. Are your friends in real life

C. Have a fun profile pic

Answers on page 143

SAFETY FIRST

BEAR IN MIND THAT THE SURVIVAL TECHNIQUES IN THIS BOOK ARE FOR USE ONLY IN EMERGENCIES. TAKE A RESPONSIBLE ADULT WITH YOU IF YOU GO ON AN EXPEDITION BECAUSE IT IS NEVER A GOOD IDEA TO UNDERTAKE ANY OF THE ACTIVITIES DESCRIBED BY YOURSELF.

WE URGE YOU AT ALL TIMES TO MAKE YOURSELF AWARE OF AND OBEY ALL LAWS AND REGULATIONS, AND RESPECT ALL RIGHTS, INCLUDING THE RIGHTS OF LANDOWNERS. OBEY ALL RELEVANT LAWS PROTECTING ANIMALS AND PLANTS, AND ALSO THOSE CONTROLLING THE CARRYING AND USE OF IMPLEMENTS SUCH AS CATAPULTS AND KNIVES.

SOME OF THE TECHNIQUES AND INSTRUCTIONS IN THIS BOOK MAY BE INAPPROPRIATE FOR PERSONS SUFFERING FROM CERTAIN PHYSICAL CONDITIONS OR HANDICAPS. ABOVE ALL, EXERCISE COMMON SENSE, PARTICULARLY WHEN FIRE OR SHARP OBJECTS ARE INVOLVED. FOLLOW SAFETY PRECAUTIONS AND ADVICE FROM RESPONSIBLE ADULTS AT ALL TIMES.

PICTURE CREDITS

ANSWERS

Pages 76–77: 1: A, 2: C, 3: B, 4: B, 5: C, 6: B, 7: C, 8: B, 9: A, 10:

Pages 110–111: 1: C, 2: A, 3: A, 4: B, 5: B, 6: C, 7: B, 8: B, 9: A, 10: C

Pages 140–141: 1: A, 2: C, 3: B, 4: A, 5: C, 6: A, 7: B, 8: C, 9: B, 10: B

INDEX